D0399937

Thoreau
ON FREEDOM

ATTENDING TO MAN

SELECTED WRITINGS BY
HENRY DAVID THOREAU

FOREWORD BY
ARUN GANDHI

EDITED BY
JEFFREY S. CRAMER

FULCRUM PUBLISHING
GOLDEN, COLORADO

Library of Congress Cataloging-in-Publication Data

Thoreau, Henry David, 1817–1862.
    Thoreau on freedom : attending to man : selected writings from Henry David Thoreau / edited by Jeffrey S. Cramer ; foreword by Arun Gandhi.
        p. cm.
Includes bibliographical references and index.
    ISBN 1-55591-478-0 (pbk. : alk. paper)
    1. Liberty. 2. Slaves—Emancipation—United States. I. Cramer, Jeffrey S., 1955- II. Title.
    HM1266 .T46 2003
    323.44—dc21   2002155161

Printed in the United States of America
0   9   8   7   6   5   4   3   2   1

Design: Nancy Duncan-Cashman
Cover image: Nancy Duncan-Cashman
Interior formatting: Fay L. Bartels

Fulcrum Publishing
16100 Table Mountain Parkway, Suite 300
Golden, Colorado 80403
(800) 992-2908 • (303) 277-1623
www.fulcrum-books.com

For Kazia and Zoë—
that they may understand

"It is our children's children who may perchance be
essentially free."
—*Thoreau Journal, 16 February 1851*

CONTENTS

FOREWORD

by Arun Gandhi

THERE CAN BE NO DOUBT that Henry David Thoreau was the father of the modern philosophy of nonviolence although he really didn't recognize it as such. The roots of the philosophy of nonviolence are, as M. K. Gandhi later said, embedded in antiquity. Thoreau practiced nonviolence largely in the form ofcivildisobedience but showed distinct awareness and concern for the most important principle of nonviolence, compassion for people in distress. Without compassion Thoreau would not have taken a stand against slavery and injustice. This is not to say that others lack compassion but generally we, the people, suppress compassion and give vent to pity. There is a very thin line that divides pity and compasion.

When we give a hungry person a piece of bread or a dollar to go and buy something to eat we are acting out of pity. We don't wish to extend ourselves but recognize the need to salve our conscience and so we give the hungry something to eat. However, if we were to act out of compassion we would then not look at our own comfort or consequences but stretch ourselves to the limit to remedy the injustice. This is what Thoreau did when he took a stand against slavery, and wrote so prolifically on the subject. Like Gandhi years later Thoreau also felt the only place for anyone who values justice is in the prison. Recall his famous conversation with Emerson when the latter came to get his friend out of prison.

"What on earth are you doing in there?" Emerson asked.

"What on earth are you doing out there?" Thoreau

retorted implying that Emerson too should be in prison if he felt slavery was an injustice.

I am sure Emerson did have strong feelings against slavery and other forms of injustices that society practices. But, like most of us, he rationalized "What can I alone do about this?" Thoreau went beyond rationalizations into deliberate action determined to suffer all consequences.

Now he did this without actually defining the rules of the philosophy of nonviolence. Civil disobedience is an integral part of the philosophy of nonviolence. One might say that Thoreau had the seed of an oak tree but had no idea what the oak would look like.

Later, when Gandhi was to define nonviolence through trial and error he realized that nonviolence was indeed a way of life. That much of the violence in human society is possible because we have divided the community to the point of a crisis and in the process dehumanized those who differ from us. This makes violence and oppression possible. So, to reverse this trend of violence one has to learn several "truths" of life. First, one must want a solution that is acceptable to all, not just to one person or party; second, one must learn not to act in a moment of anger because anything said or done at a time when one is not in control of one's mind is always going to lead to conflict; third, one must make a conscious effort to "humanize" people once again. If we are incapable of building good relationships with people that are based on sound principles they will not last long.

It is only when we dehumanize people and have no relationship with them that we are able to enslave them and subject them to inhuman treatment. Thoreau decided this was wrong and tried to educate the people through his writings. Gandhi later defined the importance of "relationship-building" in the practice of the philosophy of nonviolence. He said that relationships today, as also to some extent during Thoreau's time, were built largely on self-interest. "What will I gain from it?" is the question we always ask and if we come to the conclusion that we will gain nothing or not enough we break up the relationship without compunction.

When it is self-interest that propels the building of a relationship between humans it will last only as long as there is something to gain. In his time Thoreau saw the deterioration in relationships between people of color and race. He considered this to be injustice that no self-respecting human being should tolerate. Not taking a stand lends tacit approval to injustice and we become a part of the system. The beauty of nonviolence and civil disobedience is that one does not need a large organization or a large following to be able to take action. You can oppose injustice all by yourself. If Thoreau and Gandhi had refused to act according to their conscience we would not be today so interested in what they said and what they did. They both concluded that relationships must ideally be built on the four principles of Respect, Understanding, Acceptance and Appreciation.

Respect, we are told, is the first essential because it means not only respecting the self but respecting others and respecting the whole of creation as well. It is only if we have respect for people and for things that we will not harm or abuse them. Through respect we reach an Understanding of who we are and why are we here on earth. Everything that is created is created for a purpose so that one compliments the other. This realization that other people are born not to harm us but to enhance creation itself then we accept people as human beings and not as beasts or slaves. Through this process we finally reach the Appreciation of our own humanity.

Thoreau was moved to anger when he saw the injustices practiced by his society and he realized that anger could be used in two ways. We can abuse anger and cause violence or we can use anger intelligently and find a solution to the problem that caused the anger. Thoreau used his anger intelligently and showed the world alternate ways of dealing with injustices.

Almost a century later I learned the same lesson from Gandhi, my grandfather, who taught me that anger is like electricity: useful if used respectfully and intelligently or deadly when abused. Often we are chasing our tail so to speak. We abuse our anger causing violence and when violence overwhelms us we sue for peace. The assumption is that peace means the absence of physical violence, ignoring the existence of "passive" violence practiced individually and/or collectively. The nexus between the two is that passive violence fuels the fire of physical violence by generating anger in the victim. Since much of the fuel that ignites the fire of physical violence is provided by individual acts of passive violence, logically, "we must be the change we wish to see in the world." We must do serious introspection, acknowledge the passive and physical violence within us and learn how to use anger positively.

Thoreau's writings, like any philosophy, cannot be accepted dogmatically. It has to evolve with time and interact with constantly changing elements for it to thrive and progress. This book is offered as a first step in the proverbial thousand-mile journey. It is now up to the reader to transform this powerful message into action today so that the seed that Thoreau planted will not decay but grow into a powerful oak tree.

INTRODUCTION

by Jeffrey S. Cramer

WHAT IS FREEDOM? IS IT CHAINS, or a whip, that makes a slave? Is it the breaking of the chain, or the staying of the hand that holds the whip, that makes one free? When is it that we are truly free? These are questions Thoreau would ask himself and attempt to answer throughout his writings and they are questions that we are still asking ourselves today.

However impassioned his writings on the subject, the subject of Southern slavery was only an episode for Thoreau. Of the more than 2 million words in his journal, less than twenty thousand words are on the subject of slavery, and of those, most were written in direct response to the return of Anthony Burns to slavery in 1854 and the capture and death of John Brown in 1859. Thoreau's concerns were with something larger, more universal.

"I commonly attend more to nature than to man," Thoreau wrote in "The Last Days of John Brown." Despite his misgivings of reform and reformers, and his need to understand freedom in a wider context than the political issues of his day would allow, for a brief period the abolitionist movement could not to be ignored. As Ralph Waldo Emerson said, Thoreau was "almost equally opposed to every class of reformers. Yet he paid the tribute of his uniform respect to the Anti-Slavery party."

It was rare that the political climate of the day touched him so deeply. The issue of slavery, perhaps more than any other political or philosophical question of the time, was one not to be avoided. "As long as you know of it," Thoreau wrote to Parker Pillsbury on 10 April 1861, "you are particeps criminis."

Certainly it was a subject from which he could not escape. Thoreau's sisters and mother, his Aunt Maria, as well as Mrs. Joseph Ward and her daughter Prudence, both of whom had lived with the Thoreaus, and Lidian Emerson, were all members of the Woman's Anti-Slavery Society, which began in Concord, and discussions of slavery and abolition would have been frequent. Nathaniel P. Rogers' abolitionist paper, Herald of Freedom, was commonly read in the Thoreau household. Thoreau owned a copy of the 1842 Liberty and Anti-Slavery Song Book. The Middlesex County Anti-Slavery Society's annual convention was sometimes held in Concord, a town that was a stop on the Underground Railroad. When, in 1844, Emerson was about to give his "Address on Emancipation in the British West Indies," his first major public statement on the subject of slavery, and the selectman of the town would not permit the sexton to ring the assembly bell in the meetinghouse, Thoreau felt compelled to peal the bell himself.

Thoreau was long an advocate for individual resistance as a means to deal with political issues—"I quietly declare war with the State, after my fashion . . ."—using such weapons as non-payment of taxes, for example, following the lead of Bronson Alcott and Charles Lane. Slavery was a different concern however. It forced him to examine "The Rights and Duties of the Individual in Relation to Government," as he said in the lecture title of what was to become known simply as "Civil Disobedience."

The man who carefully praised Wendell Phillips' abolitionist efforts by emphasizing Phillips' declaration that he was not born to abolish slavery but to do right, would later write in aggressive support of John Brown's efforts, "I do not complain of any tactics that are effective of good, whether one wields the quill or the sword, but I shall not think him mistaken who quickest succeeds to liberate the slave. I will judge of the tactics by the fruit," and "I do not wish to kill or to be killed, but I can foresee circumstances in which both these things would be by me unavoidable."

Thoreau's support of John Brown has often proved a difficult period for many of Thoreau's readers. It was not that Thoreau had dismissed all that he himself believed in and spoke for, or that he was wholeheartedly endorsing the use of force. A sequence of events, culminating in the Burns and Brown affairs, would incite Thoreau to a fever pitch, causing him to question and challenge all that had come before. Although used as the spokesperson for civil disobedience or passive resistance, it would be an error to take those terms as synonymous with pacifism. Always re-evaluating, he was constantly challenging those concepts that we would now categorize unquestioningly as Thoreauvian. But for those who insist on a certain consistency in their heroes, Thoreau's support of John Brown was consistent with the military stance he offered in his early essay, "The Service," and with such statements in "Civil Disobedience" as: "When a sixth of the population of a nation which has undertaken to be the refuge of liberty are slaves, and a whole country is unjustly overrun and conquered by a foreign army, and subjected to military law, I think that it is not too soon for honest men to rebel and revolutionize." When Thoreau spoke in 1860 at a public meeting protesting the attempted arrest of Frank Sanborn in relation to his involvement with John Brown, it was reported in the Boston Journal (5 April 1860) that he advocated "resistance even to the law, when it opposed justice . . ."

Certainly Thoreau's ideas reflect the ideals on which our nation was founded. His words echo Thomas Jefferson who said

"When patience has begotten false estimates of its motives, when wrongs are pressed because it is believed they will be borne, resistance becomes morality" and "Rebellion to tyrants is obedience to God."

During his strongest period of abolitionist involvement, Thoreau felt that passivity in itself was a contribution to the institution of slavery. Withholding support is not the same as actively participating in righting a wrong. "Even voting for the right is doing nothing for it."

In November 1844, a few months after Emerson's speech, Concord lawyer and former Massachusetts Congressman Samuel Hoar was appointed to negotiate a settlement with South Carolina of an old dispute regarding the forcible taking of free black sailors off Massachusetts ships in Charleston harbor. Hoar, who had been accompanied by his daughter, Elizabeth, was forced out of Charleston under the seemingly real threat of being lynched if he remained.

In 1850 Congress adopted the Fugitive Slave Bill as part of the Missouri Compromise. It was legally incumbent for all citizens, including those in free states, to help the slave-catchers, and a one thousand dollar fine was levied on persons found helping escaped slaves. On 15 February 1851, a federal marshal seized a fugitive slave from Virginia by the name of Shadrach, who had been working in Boston as a waiter. While in the Court House that afternoon, he was rescued by two Black men, and on the following day was brought to Concord, where, with the help of the town blacksmith, Francis Bigelow, Shadrach was sent to Canada. Two months later, in April, Thomas Sims, who had escaped from Georgia, was arrested with different results. The Court House, literally bound with chains, was surrounded by a large police force. Unable to be rescued, Sims was returned to slavery.

It was the Burns case a few years later which more than any other enraged Thoreau. On 24 May 1854, fugitive slave Anthony Burns was arrested in Boston. Speeches in Fanueil Hall by Wendell Phillips and Theodore Parker incited a small band, which included Bronson Alcott and was led by the Reverend Thomas Wentworth Higginson, to attempt to batter down the doors of the Court House to free Burns. Officers armed with cutlasses held them off until military troops could be mustered to keep order. The rescue attempt having failed, Burns was placed aboard a U.S. cutter and returned to Virginia.

While the topic of slavery formed a continuous hum in the background, and the above events increased the pitch, John Brown came to Concord, first in March 1857 and again in May 1859. Thoreau, having lost his brother John and having been disappointed in his friend Emerson, finally found in Brown the transcendental hero he anticipated, a "man of rare common sense and directness of speech, as of action; a transcendentalist above all, a man of ideas and principles,—that was what distinguished him." When Brown was arrested after the raid on the federal arsenal at Harpers Ferry, it did not take long for Thoreau to turn him into a martyr who exhibited a selflessness equivalent to that of Christ.

Notwithstanding a brief disillusionment—"I subscribed a trifle when he was here three years ago, I had so much confidence in the man,—that he would do right,—but it would seem that he had not confidence enough in me, nor in anybody else that I know, to communicate his plans to us."—Thoreau found himself thinking so much about Brown that he put paper and pencil under his pillow so he could write in the dark when he couldn't sleep.

"When I reflect to what a cause this man devoted himself, and how religiously, and then reflect to what cause his judges and all who condemn him so angrily and fluently devote themselves, I see that they are as far apart as the heavens and earth are asunder."

Two weeks after Brown's raid, Thoreau was delivering his first public address on Brown. He was one of the first to speak out on Brown's behalf, unabashedly and unstintingly supportive:

I trust that you will pardon me for being here. I do not wish to force my thoughts upon you, but I feel forced myself. . . . I rejoice that I live in this age, that I am his contemporary. . . . Think of him,—of his rare qualities!—such a man as it takes ages to make, and ages to understand; no mock hero, nor the representative of any party. A man such as the sun may not rise upon again in this benighted land.

At times he may have grieved having had the subject of slavery forced into his ken—"I do not so much regret the present condition of things in this country (provided I regret it at all) as I do that I ever heard of it."—but having heard of it, the conditions and consequences of slavery infiltrated his life in such a way that the way he looked at the world, including the natural world, was being altered. Although a man "may still properly have other concerns to engage him," Thoreau found, for brief periods of time, that his own pursuits were severely interrupted. As he wrote in his journal on 16 June 1854:

I had never respected this government, but I had foolishly thought that I might manage to live here, attending to my private affairs, and forget it. For my part, my old and worthiest pursuits have lost I cannot say how much of their attraction, and I feel that my investment in life here is worth many per cent. less since Massachusetts last deliberately and forcibly restored an innocent man, Anthony Burns, to slavery.

The following day he continued in uncharacteristic despair and discouragement: "We are more of the earth, farther from heaven, these days. . . . The season of hope and promise is past; already the season of small fruits has arrived . . . We are a little saddened, because we begin to see the interval between our hopes and their fulfillment."

Unable to appreciate a "remarkable sunset" because his "mind was filled with Captain Brown," Thoreau wrote, "So great a wrong as his fate implied overshadowed all beauty in the world." Similarly, "I have been so absorbed of late in Captain Brown's fate as to be surprised whenever I detected the old routine running still,—met persons going about their affairs indifferent. It appeared strange to me that the little dipper should be still diving in the river as of yore; and this suggested that this grebe might be diving here when Concord shall be no more. Any affecting human event may blind our eyes to natural objects."

Affected as he was by these events, Thoreau's position on slavery and the Fugitive Slave Bill was more than an intellectual or moral exercise. It was an active and sincere participation. Better known for his night in jail or for ringing the church bells for Emerson's address, Thoreau was recalled by his contemporaries as a man whose disregard for personal jeopardy as well as his administration to the material needs of the fugitive slave was subtly heroic. Edward Emerson, Ralph Waldo Emerson's son, recalled:

While Henry Thoreau was in the woods, the slaves sometimes were brought to him there, but obviously there was no possible concealment in his house, so he would look after them by day, and at nightfall, get them to his mother's or another house of hiding. He was always ready to help with his service and didn't count risk, and also, although he had little money, always gave or advanced money to a slave who needed it.

And Moncure Conway recounted in his autobiography:

When I went to the house next morning, I found them all (Thoreau was then living in his father's house) in a state of excitement by reason of the arrival of a fugitive negro from the South, who had come fainting to their door about daybreak and thrown himself on their mercy. Thoreau took me in to see the poor wretch, whom I found to be a man with whose face as that of a slave in the South I was familiar. The negro was much terrified at seeing me, supposing that I was one of his pursuers. Having quieted his fears by the assurance that I too, though in a different sense, was a refugee from the bondage he was escaping, and at the same time being able to attest the negro's genuineness, I sat and watched the singularly tender and lowly devotion of the scholar to the slave. He must be fed, his swollen feet bathed, and he must think of nothing but rest. Again and again this coolest and calmest of men drew near to the trembling negro, and bade him feel at home, and have no fear that any power should again wrong him. He could not walk that day, but must mount guard over the fugitive, for slavehunters were not extinct in those days; and so I went away after a while much impressed by many little traits that I had seen as they appeared in this emergency, and not much disposed to cavil at their sources, whether Bible or Bhaghavat.

Finding himself torn between attending to nature and attending to man, Thoreau wrote to his friend, H.G.O. Blake, on 26 September 1855, mildly complaining, "I was glad to hear the other day that [T.W.] Higginson and _____ were gone to Ktaadn; it must be so much better to go to than a Woman's Rights or Abolition Convention . . . " By late 1859 it was clear to him that he had other lives to lead: "At any rate, I do not think it is sane to spend one's whole life talking or writing about this matter, and I have not done so. A man may have other affairs to attend to."

He had begun to return to the idea expressed ten years earlier in "Civil Disobedience" that "It is not a man's duty, as a matter of course, to devote himself to the eradication of any, even the most enormous wrong; he may still properly have other concerns to engage him; but it is his duty, at least, to wash his hands of it, and, if he gives it no thought longer, not to give it practically his support. If I devote myself to other pursuits and contemplations, I must first see, at least, that I do not pursue them sitting upon another man's shoulders."

There are some who may find Thoreau's talk of a personal and individual freedom as a trivializing of the fate of millions of slaves, and his turning to his personal affairs while his country headed toward civil war as arrogant and presumptuous, but Thoreau was broadening the concept of freedom to include economic, intellectual, and moral freedom, without which no one was truly free, whether called free or slave.

"Self-emancipation" was what he was striving for,

writing in his journal in 1845. Towards the end of 1860 he would be writing in his journal, coming full-circle, "Talk about slavery! It is not the peculiar institution of the South. It exists wherever men are bought and sold, wherever a man allows himself to be made a mere thing or a tool, and surrenders his inalienable rights of reason and conscience. Indeed, this slavery is more complete than that which enslaves the body alone." This was the slavery that, by example and through his writings, Thoreau tried to help eradicate: "It is hard to have a Southern overseer; it is worse to have a Northern one; but worst of all when you are yourself the slave-driver." However important to the survival of the United States as it existed in the 1860s, and however fervid his writings on the subject, the political aspect of abolitionism was an interruption to Thoreau's mission of an individual, more personal freedom. As he wrote in an 1837 letter to Orestes Brownson:

It hath not entered into the heart of man to conceive the full import of that word—Freedom—not a paltry Republican freedom, with a posse comitatus at his heels to administer it in doses as to a sick child—but a freedom proportionate to the dignity of his nature—a freedom that shall make him feel that he is a man among men, and responsible only to that Reason of which he is a particle, for his thoughts and his actions.

It would be a mistake to treat Thoreau's striving for personal freedom as self-involved or even strictly self-serving, because it is only through observing the self that we can observe society, it is through the "me" that we can understand the "not me," and it is by way of the individual the world can be changed. As Emerson wrote in "History": "Every revolution was first a thought in one man's mind, and when the same thought occurs to another man, it is the key to that era. Every reform was once a private opinion, and when it shall be a private opinion again, it will solve the problem of the age."

"We must first succeed alone that we may enjoy our success together," Thoreau wrote, insistent that individual reform was the beginning of universal reform. "Alas! This is the crying sin of our age, this want of faith in the prevalence of a man. Nothing can be effected but by one man."

Although he took this philosophical stance, trying to work out the question of freedom in his writings, Thoreau never turned his back on the black slave heading north, or abstained from any involvement in the abolitionist cause. Mrs. Edwin Bigelow told Edward Emerson in 1892 that when fugitive slaves left on the railroad from Concord, "Henry Thoreau went as escort probably more often than any other man. He would look after the tickets, &c, but in the cars did not sit with the fugitive so as not to attract attention to the companionship." Allen French, the Concord historian, wrote that "It was curious than when strange negroes took the west-bound train, Henry Thoreau was very likely to board it with them, buying tickets to Canada but returning too soon to have used them himself."

In April of 1860, federal marshals came to Concord to locate and arrest Frank Sanborn in regard to the Harper's Ferry affair. A struggle ensued during which the marshals were driven off by a combination of physical and legal means. Sanborn, armed with a revolver, spent the night in the home of George Prescott. Thoreau elected to spend the night in Sanborn's home to protect Sanborn's sister, Sarah, in case the marshals returned.

These are acts of spirit and fortitude, and perhaps what

appealed to him in John Brown was a confirmation of his own belief in the heroic individual. When Brown spoke in Concord in 1857, Emerson reported in his journal that Brown "believes on his own experience that one good, believing, strong-minded man is worth a hundred, nay twenty thousand men without character . . . & that the right men will give a permanent direction to the fortunes of a state."

To live right, to do right, and to perhaps cause others to do so also, was a goal toward which Thoreau strove. In the "Where I Lived, and What I Lived For" chapter of Walden, Thoreau wrote: "It is something to be able to paint a particular picture, or to carve a statue, and so to make a few objects beautiful; but it is far more glorious to carve and paint the very atmosphere and medium through which we look, which morally we can do. To affect the quality of the day, that is the highest of arts."

Thoreau lived in hard times, when everything that he believed and everything his country stood for was being challenged. During times of hardship or danger it is increasingly difficult to focus on anything beyond the moment. It is easy to be alert to the transient and to be inattentive to the permanent. Thoreau himself succumbed to this for a short while and it tore him away from that which he considered more pertinent work. "The worst tyrants are those which establish themselves in our own breast," William Ellery Channing wrote in his 1830 "Spiritual Freedom": "The man who wants force of principle and purpose is a slave, however free the air he breathes." To break the chains of slavery, Thoreau knew, and yet be subjected to the more subtle overseers of society, religion, economics, fear and prejudice was not equivalent to true freedom. It takes a fellowship of free individuals to create a free country.

A Note on the Texts
and the Arrangement

IN ORDER TO TRACE THOREAU'S DEVELOPMENT on the issues of freedom, as well as the historical events that motivated him, this volume is divided into four sections:

Farther from Heaven: On Slavery

Oh, Christian, Will You Send Me Back?: On the Fugitive Slave Bill

A Hero in This Field: On John Brown

Self-Emancipation: On Freedom

No attempt has been made within each section to impose a progression of thought that was not there, but to show the thought process, with its inconsistencies and meanderings. Strict chronological order has been avoided so that like-minded passages could be grouped together, much as Thoreau might have done in drafting an essay on the subject.

In order to remain as faithful to the texts cited, some of which have been published under variant editorial policies, no attempt at editorial consistency or standardization has been made.

Abbreviations used:

Correspondence: *The Correspondence of Henry David Thoreau*. Edited by Walter Harding and Carl Bode (New York: New York University Press, 1958)

First and Last Journeys: *The First and Last Journeys of Thoreau: Lately Discovered Among his Unpublished Journals and*

Manuscripts, edited by Franklin Benjamin Sanborn. (Boston: Printed exclusively for members of the Bibliophile Society, 1905)

Writings: *The Writings of Henry David Thoreau* (Boston: Houghton Mifflin, 1906)

FARTHER FROM HEAVEN: ON SLAVERY

> "Much as has been said
> about American slavery,
> I think that commonly we
> do not yet realize what slavery is."

WE HAVE NOW, FOR THE THIRD WINTER, had our spirits refreshed, and our faith in the destiny of the Commonwealth strengthened, by the presence and the eloquence of Wendell Phillips; and we wish to tender to him our thanks and our sympathy. The admission of this gentleman into the Lyceum has been strenuously opposed by a respectable portion of our fellow-citizens, who themselves, we trust,—whose descendants, at least, we know,— will be as faithful conservers of the true order, whenever that shall be the order of the day,—and in each instance the people have voted that they *would hear him*, by coming themselves and bringing their friends to the lecture-room, and being very silent that they *might* hear. We saw some men and women, who had long ago *come out, going in* once more through the free and hospitable portals of the Lyceum; and many of our neighbors confessed that they had had a "sound season" this once.

It was the speaker's aim to show what the State, and above all the Church, had to do, and now, alas! have done, with Texas and slavery, and how much, on the other hand, the individual should have to do with the Church and State. These were fair themes, and not mistimed, and his words were addressed to "fit audience, *and not* few."

We must give Mr. Phillips the credit of being a clean,

erect, and what was once called a consistent man. He at least is not responsible for slavery, nor for American Independence; for the hypocrisy and superstition of the Church, nor the timidity and selfishness of the State; nor for the indifference and willing ignorance of any. He stands so distinctly, so firmly, and so effectively alone, and one honest man is so much more than a host, that we cannot but feel that he does himself injustice when he reminds us of "the American Society, which he represents." . . .

We would fain express our appreciation of the freedom and steady wisdom, so rare in the reformer, with which he declared that he was not born to abolish slavery, but to do right.

"Wendell Phillips Before Concord Lyceum"
[*Writings IV.311–313*]

5 P.M.—Just put a fugitive slave, who has taken the name of Henry Williams, into the cars for Canada. He escaped from Stafford County, Virginia, to Boston last October; has been in Shadrach's place at the Cornhill Coffee-House; had been corresponding through an agent with his master, who is his father, about buying himself, his master asking $600, but he having been able to raise only $500. Heard that there were writs out for two Williamses, fugitives, and was informed by his fellow-servants and employer that Augerhole Burns and others of the police had called for him when he was out. Accordingly fled to Concord last night on foot, bringing a letter to our family from Mr. Lovejoy of Cambridge and another which Garrison had formerly given him on another occasion. He lodged with us, and waited in the house till funds were collected with which to forward him. Intended to dispatch him at noon through to Burlington, but when I went to buy his ticket, saw one at the depot who looked and behaved

so much like a Boston policeman that I did not venture that time. An intelligent and very well-behaved man, a mullatto.

Journal: 1 October 1851 [*Writings IX.37–38*]

About three weeks ago my indignation was roused by hearing that one of my townsmen, notorious for meanness, was endeavoring to get and keep a premium of four dollars which a poor Irish laborer whom he hired had gained by fifteen minutes' spading at our Agricultural Fair. To-night a free colored woman is lodging at our house, whose errand to the North is to get money to buy her husband, who is a slave to one Moore in Norfolk, Virginia. She persuaded Moore, though not a kind master, to buy him that he might not be sold further South. Moore paid six hundred dollars for him, but asks her eight hundred. My most natural reflection was that he was even meaner than my townsman. As mean as a slaveholder!

Journal: 1 November 1853 [*Writings XI.472*]

I lately attended a meeting of the citizens of Concord, expecting, as one among many, to speak on the subject of slavery in Massachusetts; but I was surprised and disappointed to find that what had called my townsmen together was the destiny of Nebraska, and not of Massachusetts, and that what I had to say would be entirely out of order. I had thought that the house was on fire, and not the prairie; but though several of the citizens of Massachusetts are now in prison for attempting to rescue a slave from her own clutches, not one of the speakers at that meeting expressed regret for it, not one even referred to it. It was only the disposition of some wild lands a thousand miles off which appeared to concern them. The inhabitants of Concord are not prepared to stand by one of their own bridges, but talk only of taking up a position on the highlands beyond the Yellowstone River. Our Buttricks and Davises and Hosmers are retreating thither, and I fear that they will have no Lexington Common between them and the enemy. There is not one slave in Nebraska; there are perhaps a million slaves in Massachusetts.

"Slavery in Massachusetts" [*Writings IV.388*]

What should concern Massachusetts is not the Nebraska Bill, nor the Fugitive Slave Bill, but her own slaveholding and servility. Let the State dissolve her union with the slaveholder. She may wriggle and hesitate, and ask leave to read the Constitution once more; but she can find no respectable law or precedent which sanctions the continuance of such a union for an instant.

"Slavery in Massachusetts" [*Writings IV.403*]

Lieutenant Herndon, whom our Government sent to explore the Amazon, and, it is said, to extend the area of slavery, observed that there was wanting there "an industrious and active population, who know what the comforts of life are, and who have artificial wants to draw out the great resources of the country." But what are the "artificial wants" to be encouraged? Not the love of luxuries, like the tobacco and slaves of, I believe, his native Virginia, nor the ice and granite and other material wealth of our native New England; nor are "the great resources of a country" that fertility or barrenness of soil which produces these. The chief want, in every State that I have been into, was a high and earnest purpose in its inhabitants. This alone draws out "the great resources" of Nature, and at last taxes her beyond her resources; for man naturally dies out of her. When we want culture more than potatoes, and illumination more than sugar-plums, then the great resources of a world are taxed and drawn out, and the result, or staple production, is, not slaves, nor operatives, but men,—those rare fruits called heroes, saints, poets, philosophers, and redeemers.

"Life without Principle" [*Writings IV.479–480*]

We are more of the earth, farther from heaven, these days. We live in a grosser element. We [are] getting deeper into the mists of earth. Even the birds sing with less vigor and vivacity. The season of hope and promise is past; already the season of small fruits has arrived. . . We are a little saddened, because we begin to see the interval between our hopes and their fulfillment. The prospect of the heavens is taken away, and we are presented only with a few small berries.

Journal: 17 June 1854 [*Writings XII.363–364*]

Again I scent the white water-lily, and a season I had waited for is arrived. How indispensable all these experiences to make up the summer! It is the emblem of purity, and its scent suggests it. Growing in stagnant and muddy [water], it bursts up so pure and fair to the eye and so sweet to the scent, as if to show us what purity and sweetness reside in, and can be extracted from, the slime and muck of earth. I think I have plucked the first one that has opened for a mile at least. What confirmation of our hopes is in the fragrance of the water-lily! I shall not so soon despair of the world for it, notwithstanding slavery, and the cowardice and want of principle of the North. It suggests that the time may come when man's deeds will smell as sweet. Such, then, is the odor our planet emits. Who can doubt, then, that Nature is young and sound? If Nature can compound this fragrance still annually, I shall believe her still full of vigor, and that there is virtue in man, too, who perceives and loves it. It is as if all the pure and sweet and virtuous was extracted from the slime and decay of earth and presented thus in a flower. The resurrection of virtue! It reminds me that Nature has been partner to no Missouri compromise. I scent no compromise in the fragrance of the white water-lily. In it, the sweet, and pure, and innocent are wholly sundered from the obscene and baleful. I do not scent in this the time-serving irresolution of a Massachusetts Governor, nor of a Boston Mayor. All good actions have contributed to this fragrance. So behave that the odor of your actions may enhance the general sweetness of the atmosphere, that, when I behold or scent a flower, I may not be reminded how inconsistent are your actions with it; for all odor is but one form of advertisement of a moral quality. If fair actions had not been performed, the lily would not smell sweet. The foul slime stands for the sloth and vice of man; the fragrant flower that springs from it, for the purity and courage which springs from its midst. It is these sights and sounds and fragrances put together that convince us of our immortality. No man believes against all evidence. Our external senses consent with our internal. This fragrance assures me that, though all other men fall, one shall stand fast; though a pestilence sweep over the earth, it shall at least spare one man.

Journal: 16 June 1854 [*Writings XII.352–353*]

There was wit and even poetry in the negro's answer to the man who tried to persuade him that the slaves would not be obliged to work in heaven. "Oh, you g' way, Massa. I know better. If dere 's no work for cullud folks up dar, dey 'll make some fur 'em, and if dere 's nuffin better to do, dey 'll make 'em shub de clouds along.

You can't fool this chile, Massa."

Journal: 11 January 1857 [*Writings XV.215*]

George Minott . . . Told me how Casey, who was a slave to a man—Whitney—who lived where Hawthorne owns,—the same house,—before the Revolution, ran off one Sunday, was pursued by the neighbors, and hid himself in the river up to his neck till nightfall, just across the Great Meadows. He ran through Gowing's Swamp and came back that night to a Mrs. Cogswell, who lived where Charles Davis does, and got something to eat; then cleared far away, enlisted, and was freed as a soldier after the war. Whitney's boy threw snowballs at him the day before, and finally C., who was chopping in the yard, threw his axe at him, and W. said he was an ugly nigger and he must put him in jail. He may have been twenty years old when stolen from Africa; left a wife and one child there. Used to say that he went home to Africa in the night and came back again in the morning; i.e., he dreamed of home.

Journal: 18 February 1858 [*Writings XVI.284–285*]

We hear the names of the worthies of Concord,—Squire Cuming and the rest,—but the poor slave Casey seems to have lived a more adventurous life than any of them. Squire Cuming probably never had to run for his life on the plains of Concord.

Journal: 20 February 1858 [*Writings XVI.285*]

I have always found that what are called the best of manners are the worst, for they are simply the shell without the meat. They cover no life at all. They are the universal slaveholders, who treat men as things. Nobody holds you more cheap than the man of manners.

Journal: 4 October 1859 [*Writings XVIII.370*]

As for measures to be adopted, among others I would advise abolitionists to make an earnest and vigorous and persevering an assault on the press, as they have already made, and with effect too, on the church. The church has decidedly improved within a year or two, aye, even within a fortnight; but the press is, almost without exception, corrupt. I believe that in this country the press exerts a greater and a more pernicious influence than the church. We are not a religious people, but we are a nation of politicians. We do not much care for, we do not read, the Bible, but we do care for and we do read the newspaper. It is a bible which we read every morning and every afternoon, standing and sitting, riding and walking. It is a bible which every man carries in his pocket, which lies on every table and counter, which the mail and thousands of missionaries are continuously dispersing. It is the only book which America has printed, and is capable of exerting an almost inconceivable influence for good or for bad. The editor is [a] preacher whom you voluntarily support. Your tax is commonly one cent, and it costs nothing for pew hire. But how many of these preachers preach the truth? I repeat the testimony of many an intelligent traveller, as well as my own convictions, when I say that probably no country was ever ruled by so mean a class of tyrants as are the editors of the periodical press in *this* country. Almost without exception the tone of the press is mercenary and servile. The *Commonwealth*, and the *Liberator*, are the only papers, as far as I know, which make themselves heard in condemnation of the cowardice and meanness of the authorities of Boston as lately exhibited. The other journals, almost without exception,—as the *Advertiser*, the *Transcript*, the *Journal*, the *Times*, *Bee*, *Herald*, etc.,— by their manner of referring to and speaking of the Fugitive Slave Law or the carrying back of the slave, insult the common sense of the country. And they do this for the most part, because they think so to secure the approbation of their patrons, and also, one would think, because they are not aware that a sounder sentiment prevails to any extent.

But, thank fortune, this preacher can be more easily reached by the weapons of the reformer than could the recreant priest. The *free* men of New England have only to refrain from purchasing and reading these sheets, have only to withhold their cents, to kill a score of them at once.

Journal: April 1851 [*Writings VIII. 178–180*]

Are they Americans, are they New-Englanders, are they inhabitants of Concord,—Buttricks and Davises and Hosmers by name,—who read and support the Boston *Herald*, *Advertiser*, *Traveller*, *Journal*, *Transcript*, etc., etc., *Times*? Is that the *Flag of our Union*?

Could slavery suggest a more complete servility? Is there any dust which such conduct does not lick and make fouler still with its slime? Has not the Boston *Herald* acted its part well, served its master faithfully? How could it have gone lower on its belly? How can a man stoop lower than he is low? do more than put his extremities in the place of that head he has? than make his head his *lower* extremity. And when I say the Boston *Herald* I mean the Boston press, with such few and slight exceptions as need not be made. When I have taken up this paper or the Boston *Times*, with my cuffs turned up, I have heard the gurgling of the sewer through every column; I have felt that I was handling a paper picked out of the public sewers, a leaf from the gospel of the gambling-house, the groggery, and the brothel, harmonizing with the gospel of the Merchant's Exchange.

Journal: 26 April 1851 [*Writings VIII. 181–182*]

The United States have a coffle of four millions of slaves. They are determined to keep them in this condition; and Massachusetts is one of the confederated overseers to prevent their escape. Such are not all the inhabitants of Massachusetts, but such are they who rule and are obeyed here. It was Massachusetts, as well as Virginia, that put down this insurrection at Harper's Ferry. She sent the marines there, and she will have *to pay the penalty of her sin*.

"A Plea for Captain John Brown" [*Writings IV.430–431*]

What is the character of that calm which follows when the law and the slaveholder prevail?

Journal: 19 October 1859 [*Writings XVIII.404*]

Paley, a common authority with many on moral questions, in his chapter on the "Duty of Submission to Civil Government," resolves all civil obligation into expediency. . . . But Paley appears never to have contemplated those cases to which the rule of expediency does not apply, in which a people, as well as an individual, must do justice, cost what it may. If I have unjustly wrested a plank from a drowning man, I must restore it to him though I drown myself. This, according to Paley, would be inconvenient. But he that would save his life, in such a case, shall lose it. This people must cease to hold slaves, and to make war on Mexico, though it cost them their existence as a people.

"Civil Disobedience" [*Writings IV.361–362*]

"The American Board of Commissioners for Foreign Missions," which have just met in Philadelphia, did not dare as a body to protest even against the foreign slave-trade, which even many domestic slave-traders are ready to do. And I hear of Northern men, women, and children by families buying a life-membership in this society. A life-membership in the grave! You can get buried cheaper than that.

Journal: 19 October 1859 [*Writings XVIII.407*]

. . . the representatives of so-called Christians (I refer to the Board of Commissioners for Foreign Missions), who pretend to be interested in the heathen, dare not so much as protest against the foreign slave-trade!

Journal: 21 October 1859 [*Writings XVIII.415–416*]

A government that pretends to be Christian and crucifies a million Christs every day!

Journal: 19 October 1859 [*Writings XVIII.404*]

In California and Oregon, if not nearer home, it is common to treat men exactly like deer with are hunted, and I read from time to time in Christian newspapers how many "bucks," that is, Indian men, their sportsmen have killed.

Journal: 21 October 1859 [*Writings XVIII.416–417*]

I know that most men think differently from myself; but those whose lives are by profession devoted to the study of these or kindred subjects content me as little as any. Statesmen and legislators, standing so completely within the institution, never distinctly and nakedly behold it. They speak of moving society, but have no resting-place without it. They may be men of a certain experience and discrimination, and have no doubt invented ingenious and even useful systems, for which we sincerely thank them; but all their wit and usefulness lie within certain not very wide limits.

They are wont to forget that the world is not governed by policy and expediency. Webster never goes behind government, and so cannot speak with authority about it. His words are wisdom to those legislators who contemplate no essential reform in the existing government; but for thinkers, and those who legislate for all time, he never once glances at the subject. I know of those whose serene and wise speculations on this theme would soon reveal the limits of his mind's range and hospitality. Yet, compared with the cheap professions of most reformers, and the still cheaper wisdom and eloquence of politicians in general, his are almost the only sensible and valuable words, and we thank Heaven for him. Comparatively, he is always strong, original, and, above all, practical. Still, his quality is not wisdom, but prudence. The lawyer's truth is not Truth, but consistency or a consistent expediency. Truth is always in harmony with herself, and is not concerned chiefly to reveal the justice that may consist with wrong-doing. He well deserves to be called, as he has been called, the Defender of the Constitution. There are really no blows to be given by him but defensive ones. He is not a leader, but a follower. His leaders are the men of '87. "I have never made an effort," he says, "and never propose to make an effort; I have never countenanced an effort, and never mean to countenance an effort, to disturb the arrangement as originally made, by which various States came into the Union." Still thinking of the sanction which the Constitution gives to slavery, he says, "Because it was a part of the original compact,—let it stand." Notwithstanding his special acuteness and ability, he is unable to take a fact out of its merely political relations, and behold it as it lies absolutely to be disposed of by the intellect,—what, for instance, it behoves a man to do here in America to-day with regard to slavery,—but ventures, or is driven, to make some such desperate answer as the following, while professing to speak absolutely, and as a private man,—from which what new and singular code of social duties might be inferred? "The manner," says he, "in which the governments of those States where slavery exists are to regulate it is for their own consideration, under their responsibility to their constituents, to the general laws of propriety, humanity, and justice, and to God. Associations formed elsewhere, springing from a feeling of humanity, or any other cause, have nothing whatever to do with it. They have never received any encouragement from me, and they never will."

"Civil Disobedience" [*Writings IV.383–385*]

Talk about slavery! It is not the peculiar institution of the South. It exists wherever men are bought and sold, wherever a man allows himself to be made a mere thing or a tool, and surrenders his inalienable rights of reason and conscience. Indeed, this slavery is more complete than that which enslaves the body alone. It exists in the Northern States, and I am reminded by what I find in the newspapers that it exists in Canada. I never yet met with, or heard of, a judge who was not a slave of this kind, and so the finest and most unfailing weapon of injustice. He fetches a slightly higher price than the black man only because he is a more valuable slave. It appears that a colored man killed his would-be kidnapper in Missouri and fled to Canada. The blood-hounds have tracked him to Toronto and now demand him of her judges. From all that I can learn, they are playing their parts like judges. They are servile, while the poor fugitive in their jail is free in spirit at least.

This is what a Canadian writes to the *New York Tribune*: "Our judges may be compelled to render a judgment adverse to the prisoner. Depend upon it, they will not do it unless *compelled* [his italics]*. And then the poor fellow will be taken back, and probably burned to death by the brutes of the South." Compelled! By whom? Does God compel them? or is it some other master whom they serve? Can't they hold out a little longer against the *tremendous pressure?* If they are fairly represented, I would n't trust their courage to defend a setting hen of mine against a weasel. Will this excuse avail them when the real day of judgment comes? They have not to fear the slightest bodily harm: no one stands over them with a stick or a knife even [?]. They have at the worst only to resign their places and not a mouse will squeak about it. And yet they are likely to assist in tying this victim to the stake! Would that his example might teach them to break their own fetters! They appear not to know what kind of justice that is which is to be done though the heavens fall. Better that the British Empire be destroyed than that it should help to reënslave this man!

This correspondent suggests that the "good people" of New York may rescue him as he is being carried back. There, then, is the only resort of justice,—not where the judges are, but where the mob is, where human hearts are beating, and hands move in obedience to their impulses. Perhaps his fellow-fugitives in Toronto may not feel compelled to surrender him. Justice, departing from the Canadian soil, leaves her last traces among these.

Journal: 4 December 1860 [*Writings XX.292–94*]

* Thoreau's brackets

The huckleberries, excepting the late, are now generally in blossom. . . . One of the great crops of the year. . . . The crops of oranges, lemons, nuts, and raisins, and figs, quinces, etc., etc., not to mention tobacco and the like, is of no importance to us compared with these. The berry-promising flower of the *Vaccinieæ*! This crop grows wild all over the country,—wholesome, bountiful, and free,—...and yet men—the foolish demons that they are—devote themselves to culture of tobacco, inventing slavery and a thousand other curses as the means,—with infinite pains and inhumanity go raise tobacco all their lives.

Journal: 28 May 1854 [*Writings XII.309*]

The heaven-born Numa, or Lycurgus, or Solon, gravely makes laws to regulate the exportation of tobacco. Will a divine legislator legislate for slaves, or to regulate the exportation of tobacco? What shall a State say for itself at the last day, in which this is a principal production?

Journal: July 1850 [*Writings VIII.47*]

Wait not till slaves pronounce the word
  To set the captive free,—
Be free yourselves, be not deferred,
  And farewell, slavery!

Ye are all slaves, ye have your price,
  And gang but cries to gang;
Then rise, the highest of ye rise;—
  I hear your fetters clang.

Think not the tyrant sits afar;
  In your own breasts ye have
The District of Columbia,
  And power to free the Slave.

The warmest heart the north doth breed

Is still too cold and far;
The colored man's release must come
From outcast Africa.

"Make haste and set the captive free!"
Are ye so free that cry?
The lowest depths of slavery
Leave freedom for a sigh.

What is your whole Republic worth?
Ye hold out vulgar lures;
Why will ye be disparting earth
When all of heaven is yours?

He's governed well who rules himself,
No despot vetoes him;
There's no defaulter steals his pelf,
Nor revolution grim.

'Tis neither silver, rags, nor gold,
'S the better currency;
The only specie that will hold,
Is current honesty.

The minister of state hath cares,
He cannot get release, —
Administer his own affairs,
Not settle his own peace.

'Tis easier to treat with kings

And please our country's foes,
    Than treat with Conscience of the things
        Which only Conscience knows.

There's but the party of the great,
    And party of the mean;
And if there is an Empire State,
    'Tis the upright, I ween.

[*First and Last Journeys I.137–138*]

I cannot for an instant recognize that political organization as *my* government which is the *slave's* government also.

"Civil Disobedience" [*Writings IV.360*]

Practically speaking, the opponents to a reform in Massachusetts are not a hundred thousand politicians at the South, but a hundred thousand merchants and farmers here, who are more interested in commerce and agriculture than they are in humanity, and are not prepared to do justice to the slave and to Mexico, *cost what it may*. I quarrel not with far-off foes, but with those who, near at home, coöperate with, and do the bidding of, those far away, and without whom the latter would be harmless. We are accustomed to say, that the mass of men are unprepared; but improvement is slow, because the few are not materially wiser or better than the many. It is not so important that many should be as good as you, as that there be some absolute goodness somewhere; for that will leaven the whole lump. There are thousands who are *in opinion* opposed to slavery and to the war, who yet in effect do nothing to put an end to them; who, esteeming themselves children of Washington and Franklin, sit down with their hands in their pockets, and say that they know not what to do, and do nothing; who even postpone the question of freedom to the question of free trade, and quietly read the prices-current along with the latest advices from Mexico, after dinner, and, it may be, fall asleep over them both. What is the price-current of an honest man and patriot to-day?

"Civil Disobedience" [*Writings IV.362–363*]

All voting is a sort of gaming, like checkers or backgammon, with a slight moral tinge to it, a playing with right and wrong, with moral questions; and betting naturally accompanies it. The character of the voters is not staked. I cast my vote, perchance, as I think right; but I am not vitally concerned that that right should prevail. I am willing to leave it to the majority. Its obligation, therefore, never exceeds that of expediency. Even voting *for the right* is *doing* nothing for it. It is only expressing to men feebly your desire that it should prevail. A wise man will not leave the right to the mercy of chance, nor wish it to prevail through the power of the majority. There is but little virtue in the action of masses of men. When the majority shall at length vote for the abolition of slavery, it will be because they are indifferent to slavery, or because there is but little slavery left to be abolished by their vote. *They* will then be the only slaves. Only *his* vote can hasten the abolition of slavery who asserts his own freedom by his vote.

"Civil Disobedience" [*Writings IV.363–364*]

It is not a man's duty, as a matter of course, to devote himself to the eradication of any, even the most enormous, wrong; he may still properly have other concerns to engage him; but it is his duty, at least, to wash his hands of it, and, if he gives it no thought longer, not to give it practically his support. If I devote myself to other pursuits and contemplations, I must first see, at least, that I do not pursue them sitting upon another man's shoulders.

"Civil Disobedience" [*Writings IV.365*]

As for my prospective reader, I hope that he *ignores* Fort Sumpter, & Old Abe, & all that, for that is just the most fatal and indeed the only fatal, weapon you can direct against evil ever; for as long as you *know* of it, you are *particeps criminis*. What business have you, if you are "an angel of light," to be pondering over the deeds of darkness, reading the New York Herald, & the like? I do not so much regret the present condition of things in this country (provided I regret it at all) as I do that I ever heard of it.

Letter to Parker Pillsbury, 10 April 1861 [*Correspondence 611*]

I know this well, that if one thousand, if one hundred, if ten men whom I could name,—if ten *honest* men only,—ay, if *one* HONEST man, in this State of Massachusetts, *ceasing to hold slaves*, were actually to withdraw from this copartnership, and be locked up in the county jail therefor, it would be the abolition of slavery in America. For it matters not how small the beginning may seem to be: what is once well done is done for ever. But we love better to talk about HONEST: that we say is our mission. Reform keeps many scores of newspapers in its service, but not one man. If my esteemed neighbor, the State's ambassador, who will devote his days to the settlement of the question of human rights in the Council Chamber, instead of being threatened with the prisons of Carolina, were to sit down the prisoner of Massachusetts, that State which is so anxious to foist the sin of slavery upon her sister,— though at present she can discover only an act of inhospitality to be the ground of a quarrel with her,—the Legislature would not wholly waive the subject the following winter.

"Civil Disobedience" [*Writings IV.370*]

We will quote from the same sheet [Nathaniel P. Rogers' *Herald of Freedom*] his indignant and touching satire on the funeral of those public officers who were killed by the explosion on board the Princeton, together with the President's slave; an accident which reminds us how closely slavery is linked with the government of this nation. The President coming to preside over a nation of *free* men, and the man who stands *next to him a slave*!

"Herald of Freedom" [*The Dial (April 184) 512*]

I have not so surely forseen that any Cossack or Chippeway would come to disturb the honest and simple commonwealth, as that some monster institution would at length embrace and crush its free members in its scaly folds; for it is not to be forgotten, that while the law holds fast the thief and murderer, it lets itself go loose. When I have not paid the tax which the State demanded for that protection which I did not want, itself has robbed me; when I have asserted the liberty it presumed to declare, itself has imprisoned me. Poor creature! if it knows no better I will not blame it. If it cannot live but by these means, I can. I do not wish, it happens, to be associated with Massachusetts, either in holding slaves or in conquering Mexico. I am a little better than herself in these respects.

"Monday," *A Week on the Concord and Merrimack Rivers* [*Writings I.135*]

Herein is the tragedy: that men doing outrage to their proper natures, even those called wise and good, lend themselves to perform the office of inferior and brutal ones. Hence come war and slavery in; and what else may not come in by this opening?

"Monday," *A Week on the Concord and Merrimack Rivers* [*Writings I.136*]

I do not wish to believe that the courts were made for fair weather, and for very civil cases merely; but think of leaving it to any court in the land to decide whether more than three millions of people, in this case a sixth part of a nation, have a right to be freemen or not!

"Slavery in Massachusetts" [*Writings IV.395*]

Slavery has produced no sweet-scented flower like the water-lily, for its flower must smell like itself. It will be a carrion-flower.

Journal: 17 June 1854 [*Writings XII.361*]

Slavery and servility have produced no sweet-scented flower annually, to charm the senses of men, for they have no real life: they are merely a decaying and a death, offensive to all healthy nostrils. We do not complain that they *live*, but that they do not *get buried*. Let the living bury them; even they are good for manure.

"Slavery in Massachusetts" [*Writings IV.408*]

The slave-ship is on her way, crowded with its dying victims; new cargoes are being added in mid-ocean; a small crew of slave-holders, countenanced by a large body of passengers, is smothering four millions under the hatches, and yet the politician asserts that the only proper way by which deliverance is to be obtained is by "the quiet diffusion of the sentiments of humanity," without any "outbreak." As if the sentiments of humanity were ever found unaccompanied by its deeds, and you could disperse them, all finished to order, the pure article, as easily as water with a watering-pot, and so lay the dust. What is that that I hear cast overboard? The bodies of the dead that have found deliverance. That is the way we are "diffusing" humanity, and its sentiments with it.

"A Plea for Captain John Brown" [*Writings IV.423–424*]

We seem to have forgotten that the expression "a *liberal* education" originally meant among the Romans one worthy of *free* men; while the learning of trades and professions by which to get your livelihood merely was considered worthy of *slaves* only. But taking a hint from the word, I would go a step further, and say that it is not the man of wealth and leisure simply, though devoted to art, or science, or literature, who, in a true sense, is *liberally* educated, but only the earnest and *free* man. In a slaveholding country like this, there can be no such thing as a *liberal* education tolerated by the State; and those scholars of Austria and France who, however learned they may be, are contented under their tyrannies have received only a *servile* education.

"The Last Days of John Brown" [*Writings IV.448*]

A recent English writer (De Quincey), endeavoring to account for the atrocities of Caligula and Nero, their monstrous and anomalous cruelties, and the general servility and corruption which they imply, observes that it is difficult to believe that "the descendants of a people so severe in their habits" as the Romans had been "could thus rapidly" have degenerated and that, "in reality, the citizens of Rome were at this time a new race, brought together from every quarter of the world, but especially from Asia." A vast "proportion of the ancient citizens had been cut off by the sword," and such multitudes of emancipated slaves from Asia had been invested with the rights of citizens, "that, in a single generation, Rome became almost transmuted into a baser metal." As Juvenal complained, "the Orontes . . . had mingled its impure waters with those of the Tiber." And "probably, in the time of Nero, not one man in six was of pure Roman descent." Instead of such, says another, "came Syrians, Cappadocians, Phyrgians, and other enfranchised slaves." "These in half a century had sunk so low, that Tiberius pronounced her [Rome's]* very senators to be *homines ad servitutem natos*, men born to be slaves."

So one would say, in the absence of particular genealogical evidence, that the vast majority of the inhabitants of the City of Boston, even those of senatorial dignity,—the Curtises, Lunts, Woodburys, and others,—were not descendants of the men of the Revolution,—the Hancocks, Adamses, Otises,—but some "Syrians, Cappadocians, and Phyrgians," merely, *homines ad servitutem natos,* men born to be slaves. But I would have done with comparing ourselves with our ancestors, for on the whole I believe that even they, if somewhat braver and less corrupt than we, were not men of so much principle and generosity as to go to war in behalf of another race in their midst. I do not believe that the North will soon come to blows with the South on this question. It would be too bright a page to be written in the history of the race at present.

Journal: April 1851 [*Writings VIII. 173–174*]

* Thoreau's brackets

To our disgrace we know not what to call him [Frederick Douglass], unless Scotland will lend us the spoils of one of her Douglasses, out of history or fiction, for a season, till we be hospitable and brave enough to hear his proper name,—a fugitive slave in one more sense than we; who has proved himself the possessor of a *fair* intellect, and has won a colorless reputation in these parts; and who, we trust, will be as superior to degradation from the sympathies of Freedom, as from the antipathies of slavery. When, said Mr. Phillips, he communicated to a New Bedford audience, the other day, his purpose of writing his life, and telling his name, and the name of his master, and the place he ran from, the murmur ran round the room, and was anxiously whispered by the sons of the Pilgrims, "He had better not!" and it was echoed under the shadow of Concord monument, "He had better not!"

"Wendell Philips Before Concord Lyceum" [*Writings IV.313*]

While war has given place to peace on your side, perhaps a more serious war still is breaking out here. I seem to hear its distant mutterings, though it may be long before the bolt will fall in our midst. There has not been anything which you could call union between the North and South in this country for many years, and there cannot be so long as slavery is in the way. I only wish that Northern—that any men—were better material, or that I for one had more skill to deal with them; that the north had more spirit and would settle the question at once, and here instead of struggling feebly and protractedly away off on the plains of Kansas. . . . But as for politics, what I most admire now-a-days, is not the regular governments but the irregular primitive ones, like the Vigilance committee in California and even the free state men in Kansas. They are the most divine.

Letter to Thomas Cholmondeley, 20 October 1856

[*Correspondence 435–436*]

Oh, Christian, Will You Send Me Back?: On the Fugitive Slave Bill

> "And this is called justice!"

THE LAW WILL NEVER MAKE MEN FREE; it is men who have got to make the law free. They are the lovers of law and order who observe the law when the government breaks it.

"Slavery in Massachusetts" [*Writings IV.396*]

Men of almost every degree of wit called on me in the migrating season. Some who had more wits than they knew what to do with; runaway slaves with plantation manners, who listened from time to time, like the fox in the fable, as if they heard the hounds a-baying on their track, and looked at me beseechingly, as much as to say,—"O Christian, will you send me back?"

One real runaway slave, among the rest, whom I helped forward toward the north star.

"Visitors," *Walden* [*Writings II.168–169*]

In '75 two or three hundred of the inhabitants of Concord assembled at one of the bridges with arms in their hands to assert the right of three millions to tax themselves, to have a voice in governing themselves. About a week ago the authorities of Boston, having the sympathy of many of the inhabitants of Concord, assembled in the gray of the dawn, assisted by a still larger armed force, to send back a perfectly innocent man, and one whom they knew to be innocent, into a slavery as complete as the world ever knew. Of course it makes not the least difference—

I wish you to consider this—who the man was,—whether he was Jesus Christ or another,—for inasmuch as ye did it unto the least of these his brethren ye did it unto him. Do you think *he* would have stayed here in liberty and let the black man go into slavery in his stead? They sent him back, I say, to live in slavery with other three millions—mark that—whom the same slave power, or slavish power, North and South, holds in that condition,—three millions who do not, like the first mentioned, assert the right to govern themselves but simply to run away and stay away from their prison.

Just a week afterward, those inhabitants of this town who especially sympathize with the authorities of Boston in this their deed caused the bells to be rung and the cannon to be fired to celebrate the courage and the love of liberty of those men who assembled at the bridge. As if *those* three millions had fought for the right to be free themselves, but to hold in slavery three million others. Why, gentlemen, even consistency, though it is much abused, is sometimes a virtue. Every humane and intelligent inhabitant of Concord, when he or she heard those bells and those cannon, thought not so much of the events of the 19th of April, 1775, as of the event of the 12th of April, 1851.

I wish my townsmen to consider that, whatever the human law may be, neither an individual nor a nation can ever deliberately commit the least act of injustice without having to pay the penalty for it. A government which deliberately enacts injustice, and persist in it!—it will become the laughing-stock of the world.

Much as has been said about American slavery, I think that commonly we do not yet realize what slavery is. If I were seriously to propose to congress to make mankind into sausages, I have no doubt that most would smile at my proposition and, if any believed me to be in earnest, they would think that I proposed something much worse than Congress had ever done. But, gentlemen, if any of you will tell me that to make a man into a sausage would be much worse—would be any worse—than to make him into a slave,—than it was then to enact the fugitive slave law,—I shall here accuse him of foolishness, of intellectual incapacity, of making a distinction without a difference. The one is just as sensible a proposition as the other.

When I read the account of the carrying back of the fugitive into slavery, which was read last Sunday evening, and read also what was not read here, that the man who made the prayer on the wharf was Daniel Foster of *Concord*, I could not help feeling a slight degree of pride because, of all the towns in the Commonwealth, Concord was the only one distinctly named as being represented in that tea-party, and, as she had a place in the first, so would have a place in this, the last and perhaps next most important chapter in the History of Massachusetts. But my second feeling, when I reflected how short a time that gentleman has resided in this town, was one of doubt and shame, because the *men* of Concord in recent times have done nothing to entitle them to the honor of having their town named in such a connection. . . .

It has come to this, that the friends of liberty, the friends of the slave, have shuddered when they have understood that his fate has been left to the legal tribunals, so-called, of the country to be decided. The people have no faith that justice will be awarded in such a case. The judge may decide this way or that; it is a kind of accident at best. It is evident that he is not a competent authority in so important a case. I would not trust the life of my friend to the judges of all the Supreme Courts in the world put together, to be sacrificed or saved by precedent. I would much rather trust to the sentiment of the people, which would itself be a precedent to posterity. In their vote you would get something worth having at any rate, but in the other case only the trammelled judgment of an individual, of no significance, be it which way it will.

Journal: April 1851 [*Writings VIII. 174–178*]

These days it is left to one Mr. Loring to say whether a citizen of Massachusetts is a slave or not. Does any one think that Justice or God awaits Mr. Loring's decision? Such a man's existence in this capacity under these circumstances is as impertinent as the gnat that settles on my paper. We do not ask him to make up his mind, but to make up his pack. Why, the United States Government never performed an act of justice in its life! And this unoffending citizen is held a prisoner by the United States soldier, of whom the best you can say is that he is a fool in a painted coat. Of what use a Governor or a Legislature? they are nothing but politicians. I have listened of late to hear the voice of a Governor, Commander-in-Chief of the forces of Massachusetts. I heard only the creaking of the crickets and the hum of the insects which now fill the summer air. The Governor's exploit is to review the troops on muster-days. I have seen him on horseback, with his hat off, listening to a chaplain's prayer. That is all I have ever seen of a Governor. I think that I could manage to get along without one. When freedom is most endangered, he dwells in the deepest obscurity. A distinguished clergyman once told me that he chose the profession of a clergyman because it afforded the most leisure for literary pursuits. I would recommend to him the profession of a Governor. I see the papers full of soft speeches of the mayor and the Governor and brother editors. I see the Court-House full of armed men, holding prisoner and trying a MAN, to find out if he is not really a SLAVE. It is a question about which there is great doubt.

It is really the trial of Massachusetts. Every moment that she hesitates to set this man free, she is convicted. The Commissioner on her case is God. Perhaps the most saddening aspect of the matter is the tone of almost all the Boston papers, connected with the fact that they are and have been of course sustained by a majority of their readers. They are feeble indeed, but only as sin compared with righteousness and truth. They are eminently time-serving. I have seen only the *Traveller, Journal*, and *Post*. I never look at them except at such a time as this. Their life is abject even as that of the marines. Men in any office of government are everywhere and forever politicians. Will mankind never learn that policy is not morality, that it never secures any moral right, but always considers merely what is "expedient,"—chooses the available candidate, who, when moral right is concerned, is always the devil? Witness the President of the United States. What is the position of Massachusetts? (Massa-chooses-it!) She leaves it to a Mr. Loring to decide whether one of her citizens is a freeman or a slave. What is the value of such a SHE'S FREEDOM AND PROTECTION to me? Perhaps I shall so conduct that she will one day offer me the FREEDOM OF MASSACHUSETTS in a gold casket,—made of California gold in the form of a court-house, perchance. I spurn with contempt any bribe which she or her truckling men can offer. I do not vote at the polls. I wish to record my vote here. Men profess to be surprised because the devil does not behave like an angel of light. The majority of men of the North, and of the South and East and West, are not men of principle. If they vote, they do not send men to Congress on errands of humanity; but, while their brothers and sisters are being scourged and hung for loving liberty, while (insert here all the inhumanities that pandemonium can conceive of), it is the mismanagement of wood and iron and stone and gold which concerns them. Do what you will, O Government, with my mother and brother, my father and sister, I will obey your command to the letter. It will, indeed, grieve me if you hurt them, if you deliver them to overseers to be hunted by hounds, and to be whipped to death; but, nevertheless, I will peaceably pursue my chosen calling on this fair earth, until, perhaps, one day I shall have persuaded you to relent. Such is the attitude, such are the words of Massachusetts. Rather than thus consent to establish hell upon earth,—to be a party to this establishment,—I would touch a match to blow up earth and hell together. As I love my life, I would side with the Light and let the Dark Earth roll from under me, calling my mother and my brother to follow me.

Journal: 29 May 1854 [Writings XII.313–315]

I think that recent events will be valuable as a criticism on the administration of justice in our midst, or rather as revealing what are the true sources of justice in any community. It is to some extent fatal to the courts when the people are compelled to go behind the courts. They learn that the courts are made for fair weather and for very civil cases.

Journal: April 1851 [Writings VIII.178]

I hear a good deal said about trampling this law under foot. Why, one need not go out of his way to do that. This law rises not to the level of the head or the reason; its natural habitat is in the dirt. It was born and bred, and has its life, only in the dust and mire, on a level with the feet; and he who walks with freedom, and does not with Hindoo mercy avoid treading on every venomous reptile, will inevitably tread on it, and so trample it under foot,— and Webster, its maker, with it, like the dirt-bug and its ball.

"Slavery in Massachusetts" [*Writings IV.394–395*]

Covered with disgrace, this State has sat down coolly to try for their lives the men who attempted to do its duty for it. And this is called justice! They who have shown that they can behave particularly well,—they alone are put under bonds "for their good behavior!" Such a judge and court are an impertinence. Only they are guiltless who commit the crime of contempt of such a court. It behooves every man to see that his influence is on the side of justice, and let the courts make their own characters. What is any political organization worth, when it is in the service of the devil? I see that the authorities—the Governor, Mayor, Commissioner, Marshal, etc.—are either weak or unprincipled men,—*i.e.*, well disposed but not equal to the occasion,—or else of dull moral perception, with the unprincipled and servile in their pay. All sound moral sentiment is opposed to them.

I had thought that the Governor was in some sense the executive officer of the State; that it was his business to see that the laws of the State were executed; but, when there is any special use for him, he is useless, permits the laws to go unexecuted, and is not heard from. But the worst I shall say of the Governor is that he was no better than the majority of his constituents—he was not equal to the occasion. While the whole military force of the State, if need be, is at the service of a slaveholder, to enable him to carry back a slave, not a soldier is offered to save a citizen of Massachusetts from being kidnapped. Is this what all these arms, all this "training," has been for these seventy-eight years past? What is wanted is men of principle, who recognize a higher law than the decision of the majority. The marines and the militia whose bodies were used lately were not men of sense nor of principle; in a high moral sense they were not *men* at all.

Justice is sweet and musical to hear; but injustice is harsh and discordant. The judge still sits grinding at his organ, but it yields no music, and we hear only the sound of the handle. He believes that all the music resides in the handle, and the crowd toss him their coppers just the same as before.

Journal: 9 June 1854 [*Writings XII.339–40*]

Three years ago, also, when the Sims tragedy was acted, I said to myself, There is such an officer, if not such a man, as the Governor of Massachusetts,—what has he been about the last fortnight? Has he had as much as he could do to keep on the fence during this moral earthquake? It seemed to me that no keener satire could have been aimed at, no more cutting insult have been offered to that man, than just what happened,—the absence of all inquiry after him in that crisis. The worst and the most I chance to know of him is, that he did not improve that opportunity to make himself known, and worthily known. He could at least have *resigned* himself into fame. It appeared to be forgotten that there was such a man or such an office. Yet no doubt he was endeavoring to fill the gubernatorial chair all the while. He was no Governor of mine. He did not govern me.

"Slavery in Massachusetts" [*Writings IV.390*]

Perhaps I do not know what are the duties of a Governor; but if to be a Governor requires to subject one's self to so much ignominy without remedy, if it is to put a restraint upon my manhood, I shall take care never to be Governor of Massachusetts....What I am concerned to know is, that that man's influence and authority were on the side of the slaveholder, and not of the slave,—of the guilty, and not of the innocent,—of injustice, and not of justice. I never saw him of whom I speak; indeed, I did not know that he was Governor until this event occurred. I heard of him and Anthony Burns at the same time, and thus, undoubtedly, most will hear of him. So far am I from being governed by him. I do not mean that it was anything to his discredit that I had not heard of him, only that I heard what I did.

"Slavery in Massachusetts" [*Writings IV.391–392*]

The only government that I recognize is that power that establishes justice in the land, never that which establishes injustice. Suppose that there is a private company in Massachusetts that out of its own purse and magnanimity saves all the fugitive slaves that run to us, and protects our colored fellow-citizens, and leaves the other work to the government, so called. Is not that government fast losing its occupation and becoming contemptible to mankind? If private men are obliged to perform the offices of government, to protect the weak and dispense justice, then the government becomes only a hired man, or clerk, to perform menial or indifferent services. Of course, that is but the shadow of a government, whose existence necessitates a Vigilance Committee. But such is the character of our Northern States, generally; each has its Vigilance Committee. And, to a certain extent, these crazy governments recognize and accept this relation. They say, virtually, "We'll be glad to work for you on these terms, only don't make a noise about it." Such a government is losing its power and respectability as surely as water runs out of a leaky vessel and is held by one that can contain it.

Journal: 19 October 1859 [*Writings XVIII.409–410*]

The only *free* road, the Underground Railroad, is owned and managed by the Vigilant Committee. *They* have tunnelled under the whole breadth of the land.

"A Plea for Captain John Brown" [*Writings IV.431–432*]

The effect of a good government is to make life more valuable,— of a bad government, to make it less valuable. We can afford that railroad and all merely material stock should depreciate, for that only compels us to live more simply and economically; but suppose the value of life itself should be depreciated. Every man in New England capable of the sentiment of patriotism must have lived the last three weeks with the sense of having suffered a vast, indefinite loss. I had never respected this government, but I had foolishly thought that I might manage to live here, attending to my private affairs, and forget it. For my part, my old and worthiest pursuits have lost I cannot say how much of their attraction, and I feel that my investment in life here is worth many per cent. less since Massachusetts last deliberately and forcibly restored an innocent man, Anthony Burns, to slavery. I dwelt before in the illusion that my life passed somewhere only *between* heaven and hell, but now I cannot persuade myself that I do not dwell wholly within hell. The sight of that political organization called Massachusetts is to me morally covered with scoriæ and volcanic cinders, such as Milton imagined. If there is any hell more unprincipled than our rulers and our people, I feel curious to visit it. Life itself being worthless, all things with it, that feed it, are worthless. Suppose you have a small library, with pictures to adorn the walls,—a garden laid out around,—and contemplate scientific and literary pursuits, etc., etc., and discover suddenly that your villa, with all its contents, is located in hell, and that the justice of the peace is one of the devil's angels, has a cloven foot and a forked tail,—do not these things suddenly lose their value in your eyes? Are you not disposed to sell at a great sacrifice?

I feel that, to some extent, the State has fatally interfered with my just and proper business. It has not merely interrupted me in my passage through Court Street on errands of trade, but it has, to some extent, interrupted me and every man on his onward and upward path, on which he had trusted soon to leave Court Street far behind. I have found that hollow which I had relied on for solid.

I am surprised to see men going about their business as if nothing had happened, and say to myself, "Unfortunates! they have not heard the news;" that the man whom I just met on horseback should be so earnest to overtake his newly bought cows running away,—since all property is insecure, and if they do not run away again, they may be taken away from him when he gets them. Fool! does he not know that his seed-corn is worth less this year,—that all beneficent harvests fail as he approaches the empire of hell? No prudent man will build a stone house under these circumstances, or engage in any peaceful enterprise which it requires a long time to accomplish. Art is as long as ever, but life is more interrupted and less available for a man's proper pursuits. It is time we had done referring to our ancestors. We have used up all our inherited freedom, like the young bird the albumen in the egg. It is not an era of repose. If we would save our lives, we must fight for them.

The discovery is what manner of men your countrymen

are. They steadily worship mammon—and on the seventh day curse God with a tintamarre from one end of the *Union* to the other. I heard the other day of a meek and sleek devil of a Bishop Somebody, who commended the law and order with which Burns was given up. I would like before I sit down to a table to inquire if there is one in the company who styles himself or is styled Bishop, and he or I should go out of it. I would have such a man wear his bishop's hat and his clerical bib and tucker, that we may know him.

Why will men be such fools as [to] trust to lawyers for a *moral* reform? I do not believe that there is a judge in this country prepared to decide by the principle that a law is immoral and therefore of no force. They put themselves, or rather are by character, exactly on a level with the marine who discharges his musket in any direction in which he is ordered. They are just as much tools, and as little men. . . .

P.M.—. . . There is a cool east wind,—and has been afternoons for several days, —which has produced a very thick haze or a fog. I find a tortoise egg on this peak at least sixty feet above the pond. There is a fine ripple and sparkle on the pond, seen through the mist. But what signifies the beauty of nature when men are base? We walk to lakes to see our serenity reflected in them. When we are not serene, we go not to them. Who can be serene in a country where both rulers and ruled are without principle? The remembrance of the baseness of politicians spoils my walks. My thoughts are murder to the State; I endeavor in vain to observe nature; my thoughts involuntarily go plotting against the State. I trust that all just men will conspire.

Journal: 16 June 1854 [*Writings XII.355–358*]

The judges and lawyers, and all men of expediency, consider not whether the Fugitive Slave Law is right, but whether it is what they call constitutional. They try the merits of the case by a very low and incompetent standard. Pray, is virtue constitutional, or vice? Is equity constitutional, or iniquity? It is as impertinent, in important moral and vital questions like this, to ask whether a law is constitutional or not, as to ask whether it is profitable or not. They persist in being the servants of man, and the worst of men, rather than the servants of God. Sir, the question is not whether you or your grandfather, seventy years ago, entered into an agreement to serve the devil, and that service is not accordingly now due; but whether you will not now, for once and at last, serve God,—in spite of your own past recreancy or that of your ancestors,—and obey that eternal and only just Constitution which he, and not any Jefferson or Adams, has written in your being. Is the Constitution a thing to live by? or die by? No, as long as we are alive we forget it, and when we die we have done with it. At most it is only to swear by. While they are hurrying off Christ to the cross, the ruler decides that he cannot *constitutionally* interfere to save him. The Christians, now and always, are they who obey the higher law, who discover it to be according to their constitution to interfere. They at least cut off the ears of the police; the others pocket the thirty pieces of silver. This was meaner than to crucify Christ, for he could better take care of himself.

Journal: 17 June 1854 [*Writings XII.362–363*]

Massachusetts sits waiting his decision, as if the crime were not already committed. The crime consists first of all and chiefly in her permitting an innocent man to be tried for more than his life,— for his liberty. They who talk about Mr. Loring's decision, and not about their own and the State's consenting that he shall be the umpire in such a case, waste time in words and are weak in the head, if not in the heart alone [*sic*].

(June 9th, continued.)—The amount of it is, if the majority vote the devil to be God, the minority will live and behave accordingly, and obey the successful candidate, trusting that some time or other, by some Speaker's casting-vote, they may reinstate God again. Some men act as if they believed that they could safely slide down-hill a little way,—or a good way,—and would surely come to a place, by and by, whence they could slide up again. This is *expediency*, or choosing that course which offers the fewest obstacles to the feet (of the slider). But there is no such thing as accomplishing a moral reform by the use of expediency or policy. There is no such thing as sliding up-hill. In morals the only sliders are backsliders.

Let the judge and the jury, and the sheriff and the jailer, cease to act under a corrupt government,—cease to be tools and become men.

Certainly slavery, and all vice and iniquity, have not had power enough to create any flower thus annually to charm the senses of men. It has no life. It is only a constant decaying and a death, offensive to all healthy nostrils. The unchangeable laws of the universe, by a partial obedience to which even sin in a measure succeeds, are all on the side of the just and fair. It is his few good qualities misallied which alone make the slaveholder at all to be feared; it is because he is in some respects a better man than we.

Why, who are the real opponents of slavery? The slaveholders know, and I know. Are they the governors, the judges, the lawyers, the politicians? Or are they Garrison, Phillips, Parker &

Co.? The politicians do now, and always will, instinctively stand aloof from such.

Journal: 17 June 1854 [Writings XII.364–366]

Massachusetts sat waiting Mr. Loring's decision, as if it could in any way affect her own criminality. Her crime, the most conspicuous and fatal crime of all, was permitting him to be the umpire in such a case. It was really the trial of Massachusetts. Every moment that she hesitated to set this man free, every moment that she now hesitates to atone for her crime, she is convicted.

"Slavery in Massachusetts" [Writings IV.393–394]

What we want is not mainly to colonize Nebraska with free men, but to colonize Massachusetts with free men,—to be free ourselves. As the enterprise of a few individuals, that is brave and practical; but as the enterprise of the State, it is cowardice and imbecility. What odds where we squat, or how much ground we cover? It is not the soil that we would make free, but men.

As for asking the South to grant us the trial by jury in the case of runaway slaves, it is as if, seeing a righteous man sent to hell, we should run together and petition the devil first to grant him a trial by jury, forgetting that there is another power to be petitioned, that there is another law and other precedents.

Journal: 18 June 1854 [Writings XII.367]

It is not any such free-soil party as I have seen, but a free-man party,—i.e. a party of free men,—that is wanted. It is not any politicians, even the truest and soundest, but, strange as it may sound, even godly men, as Cromwell discovered, who are wanted to fight this battle,—men not of policy but of probity. Politicians!

I have looked into the eyes of two or three of them, but I saw nothing there to satisfy me. They will vote for my man to-morrow if I will vote for theirs to-day. They will whirl round and round, not only horizontally like weathercocks, but vertically also.

My advice to the State is simply this: to dissolve her union with the slaveholder instantly. She can find no respectable law or precedent which sanctions its continuance. And to each inhabitant of Massachusetts, to dissolve his union with the State, as long as she hesitates to do her duty.

Journal: 18 June 1854 [*Writings XII.370*]

Show me a free state, and a court truly of justice, and I will fight for them, if need be; but show me Massachusetts, and I refuse her my allegiance, and express contempt for her courts.

"Slavery in Massachusetts" [*Writings IV.404–405*]

Nowadays, men wear a fool's cap, and call it a liberty-cap. I do not know but there are some who, if they were tied to a whipping-post, and could but get one hand free, would use it to ring the bells and fire the cannons to celebrate *their* liberty. So some of my townsmen took the liberty to ring and fire. That was the extent of their freedom; and when the sound of the bells died away, their liberty died away also; when the powder was all expended, their liberty went off with the smoke.

"Slavery in Massachusetts" [*Writings IV.393*]

A Hero in This Field: On John Brown

"I rejoice that I live in this age,
that I was his contemporary."

I SPOKE TO MY TOWNSMEN LAST EVENING on "The character of Capt. Brown, now in the clutches of the slaveholder." I should like to speak to any company in Worcester who may wish to hear me, & will come, if only my expenses are paid. I think that we should express ourselves at once, while Brown is alive. The sooner the better.

Letter to H.G.O. Blake, 31 October 1859 [*Correspondence 563*]

It galls me to listen to the remarks of craven-hearted neighbors who speak disparagingly of Brown because he resorted to violence, resisted the government, threw his life away!—what way have they thrown their lives, pray?—neighbors who would praise a man for attacking singly an ordinary band of thieves or murderers. Such minds are not equal to the occasion. They preserve the so-called peace of their community by deeds of petty violence every day. Look at the policeman's billy and handcuffs! Look at the jail! Look at the gallows! Look at the chaplain of the regiment! We are hoping only to live safely on the outskirts of *this* provisional army. So they defend themselves and our hen-roosts, and maintain slavery.

There sits a tyrant holding fettered four millions of slaves. Here comes their heroic liberator; if he falls, will he not still live?

Journal: 19 October 1859 [*Writings XVIII.401–402*]

Our foes are in our midst and all about us. Hardly a house but is divided against itself. For our foe is the all but universal wooden-ness (both of head and heart), the want of vitality, of man,—the effect of vice,—whence are begotten fear and superstition and bigotry and persecution and slavery of all kinds. Mere figure-heads upon a hulk, with livers in the place of hearts. A church that can never have done with excommunicating Christ while it exists. Our plains were overrun the other day with a flock of adjutant-generals, as if a brood of cockerels had been let loose there, wait-ing to use their spurs in what sort of glorious cause, I ask. What more probable in the future, what more certain heretofore, than in grinding in the dust four hundred thousands of feeble and timid men, women, and children? The United States exclaims: "Here are four millions of human creatures which we have stolen. We have abolished among them the relations of father, mother, children, wife, and we mean to keep them in this condition. Will you, O Massachusetts, help us to do so?" And Massachusetts promptly answers, "Aye!"

Journal: 19 October 1859 [*Writings XVIII.404*]

The momentary charge at Balaclava, in obedience to a blundering command,—proving what a perfect machine the soldier is—has been celebrated by a poet laureate; but the steady and for the most part successful charge against the legions of Slavery kept up for some years in Kansas by John Brown in obedience to an infinitely higher command is unsung,—as much more memorable than that as an intelligent and conscientious man is superior to a machine.

Journal: 19 October 1859 [*Writings XVIII.405*]

Some eighteen hundred years ago Christ was crucified; this

morning, perhaps, John Brown was hung. These are the two ends of a chain which I rejoice to know is not without its links.

Journal: 19 October 1859 [*Writings XVIII. 406*]

It is mentioned against him and as an evidence of his insanity, "a conscientious man, very modest in his demeanor, that he was apparently inoffensive, until the subject of slavery was introduced, when he would exhibit a feeling of indignation unparalleled." (*Boston Journal*, October 21, 1859.)

Journal: 19 October 1859 [*Writings XVIII. 407*]

When a man stands up serenely against the condemnation and vengeance of mankind, rising above them literally by a whole body,—though he were a slave, though he were a freeman, though he were of late the vilest murderer, who has settled that matter with himself,—the spectacle is a sublime one!—did n't ye know it, ye Garrisons, ye Buchanans, ye politicians, attorney-generals?— and we become criminal in comparison. Do yourselves the honor to recognize him. *He* needs none of your respect. What though he did not belong to your clique!

Journal: 19 October 1859 [*Writings XVIII. 408*]

What a contrast, when we turn to that political party which is so anxiously shaking its skirts clean of him and his friends and looking round for some available slaveholder to be its candidate!

Journal: 19 October 1859 [*Writings XVIII. 408*]

Insane! A father and seven sons, and several more men besides,— as many, at least, as twelve disciples,—all struck with insanity at once; while the sane tyrant holds with a firmer gripe than ever his four millions of slaves, and a thousand sane editors, his abettors, are saving their country and their bacon! Just as insane as were their efforts in Kansas. Ask the tyrant who is his most dangerous foe, the sane man or the insane.

If some Captain Ingraham threatens to fire into an Austrian vessel, we clap our hands all along the shore. It won't hit us; it won't disturb our tyranny. But let a far braver than he attack the Austria within us, we turn, we actually *fire* those same guns upon him, and cry, "Insane."

Journal: 21 October 1859 [*Writings XVIII.411–412*]

And in what a sweet, kindly strain he proceeds, addressing those who held him prisoner: "I think, my friends, you are guilty of a great wrong against God and humanity, and it would be perfectly right for any one to interfere with you so far as to free those you willfully and wickedly hold in bondage."

Journal: 21 October 1859 [*Writings XVIII.415*]

I do not complain of any tactics that are effective of good, whether one wields the quill or the sword, but I shall not think him mistaken who quickest succeeds to liberate the slave. I will judge of the tactics by the fruit.

Journal: 21 October 1859 [*Writings XVIII.417*]

I rejoice that I live in this age, that I was his contemporary.

Journal: 22 October 1859 [*Writings XVIII.421*]

For once the Sharp's rifle and the revolver were employed in a righteous cause. The tools were in the hands of one who could use them. I know that the mass of my neighbors think that the only righteous use that can be made of them is to fight duels with them when we are insulted by other nations, or hunt Indians, or shoot fugitive slaves with them.

Journal: 22 October 1859 [*Writings XVIII.422*]

It was his peculiar doctrine that a man has a perfect right to interfere by force with the slaveholder, in order to rescue the slave. I agree with him. They who are continually shocked by slavery have some right to be shocked by the violent death of the slaveholder, but no others. Such will be more shocked by his life than by his death. I shall not be forward to think him mistaken in his method who quickest succeeds to liberate the slave. I speak for the slave when I say that I prefer the philanthropy of Captain Brown to that philanthropy which neither shoots me nor liberates me.

"A Plea for Captain John Brown" [*Writings IV.433*]

The question is not about the weapon, but the spirit in which you use it.

Journal: 22 October 1859 [*Writings XVIII.422*]

Though you may not approve of his methods or his principles, cease to call names, to cry mad dog. The method is nothing; the spirit is all in all. It is the deed, the devotion, the soul of the man. For you this is at present a question of magnanimity. If the schoolboy, forgetting himself, rushed to the rescue of his drowning playmate, what though he knock down somebody on his way, what though he does not go to the same church with you, or his father belong to the same political party! Would you not like to claim kindred with him in this, though in no other thing he is like, or likely, to you?

Journal: 22 October 1859 [*Writings XVIII.422–423*]

Think of him,—of his rare qualities!—such a man as it takes ages to make, and ages to understand; no mock hero, not the representative of any party. A man such as the sun may never rise upon again in this benighted land, to whose making went the costliest material, the finest adamant, the purest gold; sent to be the redeemer of those in captivity;—and the only use to which you can put him, after mature deliberation, is to hang him at the end of a rope. I need not describe him. He has stood where I now stand; you have all seen him. You who pretend to care for Christ crucified, consider what you are about to do to him who offered himself to be the savior of four millions of men!

Journal: 22 October 1859 [*Writings XVIII.424*]

The preachers, the Bible men, they who talk about principle and doing to others as you would that they should do unto you,—how could they fail to recognize him, by far the greatest preacher of the them all, with the Bible on his lips, and in his acts, the embodiment of principle, who actually carried out the golden rule? All whose moral sense is aroused, who have a calling from on high to preach, have sided with him. It may prove the occasion, if it has not proved it already, of a new sect of *Brownites* being formed in our midst.

I see now, as he saw, that he was not to be pardoned or rescued by men. That would have been to disarm him, to restore to him a material weapon, a Sharp's rifle, when he had taken up the sword of the spirit,—the sword with which he has really won his greatest and most memorable victories. Now he has not laid aside the sword of the spirit. He is pure spirit himself, and his sword is pure spirit also.

On the day of his translation, I heard, to be sure, that he

was hung, but I did not know what that meant,—and I felt no sorrow on his account; but not for a day or two did I even *hear* that he was dead, and not after any number of days shall I believe it. Of all the men who are said to be my contemporaries, it seems to me that John Brown is the only one who *has not* died. I meet him at every turn. He is more alive than ever he was. He is not confined to North Elba nor to Kansas. He is no longer working in secret only. John Brown has earned immortality.

Men have been hung in the South before for attempting to rescue slaves, and the North was not much stirred by it. Whence, then, this wonderful difference? We were not so sure of their devotion to principle. We have made a subtle distinction, have forgotten human laws, and do homage to an idea. The North is suddenly all Transcendental. It goes behind the human law, it goes behind the apparent failure, and recognizes eternal justice and glory.

It is more generous than the spirit which actuated our forefathers, for it is a revolution in behalf of another, and an oppressed, people.

Journal: 5 December 1859 [*Writings XIX. 6–7*]

Most Northern men, and not a few Southern ones, have been wonderfully stirred by Brown's behavior and words. They have seen or felt that they were great, heroic, noble, and that there has been nothing quite equal to them in this country, if in the recent history of the world.

Journal: 6 December 1859 [*Writings XIX. 12*]

I should say that he was an old-fashioned man in his respect for the Constitution and the Declaration of Independence, and his faith in the permanence of this Union. Slavery he saw to be wholly opposed to all of these, and he was its determined foe.

Journal: 22 October 1859 [*Writings XVIII.427*]

When a government puts forth its strength on the side of injustice, as ours to maintain slavery and kill the liberators of the slave, it reveals itself a merely brute force, or worse, a demoniacal force. It is the head of the Plug-Uglies. It is more manifest than ever that tyranny rules. I see this government to be effectually allied with France and Austria in oppressing mankind. There sits a tyrant holding fettered four millions of slaves; here comes their heroic liberator. This most hypocritical and diabolical government looks up from its seat on the gasping four millions, and inquires with an assumption of innocence: "What do you assault me for? Am I not an honest man? Cease agitation on this subject, or I will make a slave of you, too, or else hang you."

"A Plea for Captain John Brown" [*Writings IV.429*]

I do not believe in lawyers, in that mode of attacking or defending a man, because you descend to meet the judge on his own ground, and, in cases of the highest importance, it is of no consequence whether a man breaks a human law or not. Let lawyers decide trivial cases. Business men may arrange that among themselves. If they were the interpreters of the everlasting laws which rightfully bind man, that would be another thing. A counterfeiting law-factory, standing half in a slave land and half in a free! What kind of laws for free men can you expect from that?

"A Plea for Captain John Brown" [*Writings IV.438*]

All through the excitement occasioned by Brown's remarkable

attempt and subsequent behavior, the Massachusetts Legislature, not taking any steps for the defense of her citizens who are likely to be carried to Virginia as witnesses and exposed to the violence of a slaveholding mob, is absorbed in a liquor-agency question. That has, in fact, been the all-absorbing question with it!! I am sure that no person up to the occasion, or who perceived the significance of the former event, could at present attend to this question at all. As for the Legislature, bad spirits occupied their thoughts.

Journal: 15 November 1859 [*Writings XVIII.445*]

I am one of a committee of four, *viz.* Simon Brown (Ex-Lieutenant-Governor), R. W. Emerson, myself, and John Keyes (late High Sheriff), instructed by a meeting of citizens to ask liberty of the selectmen to have the bell of the first parish tolled at the time Captain Brown is being hung, and while we shall be assembled in the town house to express our sympathy with him. I applied to the selectmen yesterday. Their names are George M. Brooks, Barzillai Hudson, and Julius Smith. After various delays they at length answer me to-night that they "are uncertain whether they have any control over the bell, but that, *in any case*, they will not give their consent to have the bell tolled." Beside their private objections, they are influenced by the remarks of a few individuals. Dr. Bartlett tells me that Rockwood Hoar said he "hoped no such foolish thing would be done," and he also named Stedman Buttrick, John Moore, Cheney (and others added Nathan Brooks, senior, and Francis Wheeler) as strongly opposed to it; said that he had heard "five hundred" (!) damn me for it, and that he had no doubt that if it were done some counter-demonstration would be made, such as firing minute-guns. The doctor himself is more excited than anybody, for he has the minister under his wing. Indeed, a considerable part of Concord are in the condition of Virginia to-day,—afraid of their own shadows.

Journal: 30 November 1859 [*Writings XVIII. 457–458*]

An apothecary in New Bedford told R. the other day that a man (a Mr. Leonard) of Springfield told him that he once attended a meeting in Springfield where a woman was exhibited as in a mesmeric state, insensible to pain,—a large and fleshy woman,— and the spectators were invited to test her condition with pins or otherwise. After some had tried, one among them came forward with a vial of cowage, and, after stating to the company that it would produce intolerable irritation in the skin, he proceeded to rub a little on the woman's bare arm and on her neck. She imme- diately winced under it, whereupon he took out another vial containing sweet oil, and, applying a little of that, relieved her. He then stated that any one present might apply to his skin as much as he pleased. Some came forward and he laid bare his breast and when they applied it sparingly and hesitatingly, he said, "Rub away, gentlemen,—as much as you like," and he betrayed no sign of irritation. That man was John Brown.

Journal: 18 November 1859 [*Writings XVIII. 449*]

I do not believe in erecting statues to those who still live in our minds and hearts, whose bones have not yet crumbled in the earth around us, but I would rather see the statue of John Brown in the Massachusetts State-House yard than that of any other man whom I know.

Journal: 19 October 1859 [*Writings XVIII. 408*]

I foresee the time when the painter will paint that scene, no longer going to Rome for a subject; the poet will sing it; the historian record it; and, with the Landing of the Pilgrims and the Declaration of Independence, it will be the ornament of some future national gallery, when at least the present form of slavery shall be no more here.

"A Plea for Captain John Brown" [*Writings IV.440*]

What shall we think of a government to which all the truly brave and just men in the land are enemies, standing between it and those whom it oppresses? Do not we Protestants know the likeness of Luther, Fox, Bunyan, when we see it?

Journal: 21 October1859 [*Writings XVIII.416*]

A whole nation will for ages cling to the memory of its Arthur, or other imaginary hero, who perhaps never assailed its peculiar institution or sin, and, being imaginary, never failed, when they are themselves the very freebooters and craven knights whom he routed, while they forget their real heroes.

Journal: 19 October 1859 [*Writings XVIII.405*]

If any person, in a lecture or a conversation, should now cite any ancient example of heroism, such as Cato, or Tell, or Winkelried, passing over the recent deeds and words of John Brown, I am sure that it would be felt by any intelligent audience of Northern men to be tame and inexcusably far-fetched.

Journal: 15 November 1859 [*Writings XVIII.445*]

I know that there have been a few heroes in the land, but no man has ever stood up in America for the dignity of human nature so devotedly, persistently, and so effectively as this man. . . .

Ethan Allen and Stark, though worthy soldiers in their day, were rangers in a far lower field and in a less important cause.

Journal: 21 October 1859 [*Writings XVIII.413–414*]

They (Allen and Stark) may have possessed some of his love of liberty, indignation, and courage to face their country's foes, but they had not the rare qualities—the peculiar courage and self-reliance—which could enable them to face their country itself, and all mankind, in behalf of the oppressed.

Journal: 22 October 1859 [*Writings XVIII.433*]

He was like the best of those who stood at our bridge once, on Lexington Common, and on Bunker Hill, only he was firmer and higher-principled than any that I chance to have heard of as there.

Journal: 22 October 1859 [*Writings XVIII.436*]

Another neighbor asks, Yankee-like, "What will *he* gain by it?" as if he expected to fill his pockets by this enterprise. They have no idea of gain but in this worldly sense. If it does not lead to a surprise party, if he does not get a new pair of boots and a vote of thanks, it must be a failure. Such do not know that like the seed is the fruit, and that, in the moral world, when good seed is planted, good fruit is inevitable and does not depend on our watering and cultivating; that when you plant, or bury, a hero in this field, a crop of heroes is sure to spring up.

Journal: 19 October 1859 [*Writings XVIII.406*]

"But he won't gain anything." Well, no! I don't suppose he could get four-and-sixpence a day for being hung, take the year round. But then he stands a chance to save a considerable part of his soul,—and such a soul!, —when you do not.

Journal: 21 October 1859 [*Writings XVIII.414–415*]

Editors persevered for a good while in saying that Brown was crazy; but at last they said only that it was "a crazy scheme," and the only evidence brought to prove it was that it cost him his life. I have no doubt that if he had gone with five thousand men, liberated a thousand slaves, killed a hundred or two slaveholders, and had as many more killed on his own side, but not lost his own life, these same editors would have called it by a more respectable name. Yet he has been far more successful than that. He has liberated many thousands of slaves, both North and South. They seem to have known nothing about living or dying for a principle.

["The Last Days of John Brown" *Writings IV.445–446*]

SELF-EMANCIPATION: ON FREEDOM

"It hath not entered into the heart
of man to conceive
the full import of that word—
Freedom—"

I WONDER MEN CAN BE SO FRIVOLOUS almost as to attend to the gross form of negro slavery, there are so many keen and subtle masters who subject us both. Self-emancipation in the West Indies of a man's thinking and imagining provinces, which should be more than his island territory,—one emancipated heart and intellect! It would knock off the fetters from a million slaves.

Journal: 6 July 1845 [*Writings VII.362–363*]

For a man to act himself, he must be perfectly free; otherwise he is in danger of losing all sense of responsibility or of self-respect.

Letter to Helen Thoreau, 27 October 1837
[*Correspondence 15*]

I wish to speak a word for Nature, for absolute freedom and wildness, as contrasted with a freedom and culture merely civil . . .

"Walking" [*Writings V.205*]

SPECULATION

We may believe it, but never do we live a quiet, free life, such as Adam's, but are enveloped in an invisible network of speculations. Our progress is only from one such speculation to another, and only at rare intervals do we perceive that it is no progress.

Could we for a moment drop this by-play, and simply wonder, without reference or inference!

Journal: 7 December 1838 [*Writings VII. 61*]

The world is a fit theater to-day in which any part may be acted. There is this moment proposed to me every kind of life that men lead anywhere, or that imagination can paint. By another spring I may be a mail-carrier in Peru, or a South African planter, or a Siberian exile, or a Greenland whaler, or a settler on the Columbia river, or a Canton merchant, or a soldier in Florida, or a mackerel-fisher off Cape Sable, or a Robinson Crusoe in the Pacific, or a silent navigator of any sea. So wide is the choice of parts, what a pity if the part of Hamlet be left out!

I am freer than any planet; no complaint reaches round the world. I can move away from public opinion, from government, from religion, from education, from society. Shall I be reckoned a ratable poll in the county of Middlesex, or be rated at one spear under the palm trees of Guinea? Shall I raise corn and potatoes in Massachusetts, or figs and olives in Asia Minor? sit out the day in my office in State Street, or ride it out on the steppes of Tartary? For my Brobdingnag I may sail to Patagonia; for my Lilliput, to Lapland. In Arabia and Persia, my day's adventures will surpass the Arabian Nights' Entertainments. I may be a logger on the head waters of the Penobscot, to be recorded in fable hereafter as an amphibious river-god, by as sounding a name as Triton or Proteus; carry furs from Nootka to China, and so be more renowned than Jason and his golden fleece; or go on a South Sea exploring expedition, to be hereafter recounted along with the periplus of Hanno. I may repeat the adventures of Marco Polo or Mandeville.

These are but few of my chances, and how many more things may I do with which there are none to be compared!

Journal: 21 March 1840 [*Writings VII.129–130*]

The other day I rowed in my boat a free, even lovely young lady, and, as I plied the oars, she sat in the stern, and there was nothing but she between me and the sky. So might all our lives be picturesque if they were free enough, but mean relations and prejudices intervene to shut out the sky, and we never see a man as simple and distinct as the man-weathercock on a steeple.

Journal: 19 June 1840 [*Writings VII.144*]

I must not lose any of my freedom by being a farmer and landholder. Most who enter on any profession are doomed men. The world might as well sing a dirge over them forthwith. The farmer's muscles are rigid. He can do one thing long, not many well. His pace seems determined henceforth; he never quickens it. A very rigid Nemesis is his fate. When the right wind blows or a star calls, I can leave this arable and grass ground, without making a will or settling my estate. I would buy a farm as freely as a silken streamer. Let me not think my front widows must face east henceforth because a particular hill slopes that way. My life must undulate still. I will not feel that my wings are clipped when once I have settled on ground which the law calls my own, but find new pinions grown to the old, and talaria to my feet beside.

Journal: 27 March 1841 [*Writings VII.241–242*]

AT R.W.E'S.
The charm of the Indian to me is that he stands free and unconstrained in Nature, is her inhabitant and not her guest, and wears

her easily and gracefully. But the civilized man has the habits of the house. His house is a prison in which he finds himself oppressed and confined, not sheltered and protected. He walks as if he sustained the roof; he carries his arms as if the walls would fall in and crush him, and his feet remember the cellar beneath. His muscles are never relaxed. It is rare that he overcomes the house, and learns to sit at home in it, and roof and floor and walls support themselves, as the sky and trees and earth.

Journal: 26 April 1841 [*Writings VII.253*]

I have been your pensioner for nearly two years, and still left free as under the sky.

Letter to Ralph Waldo Emerson, 24 January 1843
[*Correspondence 78*]

I never met a man who cast a free and healthy glance over life . . .

Journal: 1 August 1841 [*Writings VII.265*]

Perhaps I should give some account of myself. I would make education a pleasant thing both to the teacher and the scholar. This discipline, which we allow to be the end of life, should not be one thing in the schoolroom, and another in the street. We should seek to be fellow students with the pupil, and we should learn of, as well as with him, if we would be most helpful to him. But I am not blind to the difficulties of the case; it supposes a degree of freedom which rarely exists. It hath not entered into the heart of man to conceive the full import of that word—Freedom—not a paltry Republican freedom, with a *posse comitatus* at his heels to administer it in doses as to a sick child—but a freedom proportionate to the dignity of his nature—a freedom that shall make him feel that he is a man among men, and responsible only to that Reason of which he is a particle, for his thoughts and his actions.

Letter to Orestes Brownson, 30 December 1837
[*Correspondence 20*]

I dwell as much aloof from society as ever: find it just as impossible to agree in opinion with the most intelligent of my neighbors; they not having improved one jot, nor I either. I am still immersed in nature, have much of the time a living sense of the breadth of the field on whose verge I dwell. The *great west* and *north west* stretching on infinitely far and grand and wild, qualifying all our thoughts. That is the only America I know. I prize this western reserve chiefly for its intellectual value. That is the road to new life and freedom . . .

Letter to Thomas Cholmondeley, 20 October 1856
[*Correspondence 436*]

Paddling along the eastern side of the lake in the still of the morning, we soon saw a few sheldrakes, which the Indian called *Shecorways*, and some peetweets, *Naramekechus*, on the rocky shore; we also saw and heard loons, *Medawisla*, which he said was a sign of wind. It was inspiriting to hear the regular dip of the paddles, as if they were our fins or flippers, and to realize that we were length fairly embarked. We who had felt strangely as stage-passengers and tavern-lodgers were suddenly naturalized there and presented with the freedom of the lakes and the woods.

"The Allegash and East Branch," *The Maine Woods*
[*Writings III. 182*]

This hunter, who was a quite small, sunburnt man, having already carried his canoe over, and baked his loaf, had nothing so interesting and pressing to do as to observe our transit. He had been out a month or more alone. How much more wild and adventurous his life than that of the hunter in Concord woods, who gets back to his house and the mill-dam every night! Yet they in the towns who have wild oats to sow commonly sow them on cultivated and comparatively exhausted ground. And as for the rowdy world in the large cities, so little enterprise has it that it never adventures in this direction, but like vermin clubs together in alleys and drinking-saloons, its highest accomplishment, perchance, to run beside a fire-engine and throw brickbats. But the former is comparatively an independent and successful man, getting his living in a way that he likes, without disturbing his human neighbors. How much more respectable also is the life of the solitary pioneer or settler in these, or any woods,—having real difficulties, not of his own creation, drawing his subsistence directly from nature,—than that of the helpless multitudes in the towns who depend on gratifying the extremely artificial wants of society and are thrown out of employment by hard times!

"The Allegash and East Branch," *The Maine Woods*
[*Writings III.269–270*]

Being now fairly in the stream of this week's commerce, we began to meet with boats more frequently, and hailed them from time to time with the freedom of sailors. The boatmen appeared to lead an easy and contented life, and we thought that we should prefer their employment ourselves to many professions which are much more sought after. They suggested how few circumstances are necessary to the well-being and serenity of man, how indifferent all employments are, and that any may seem noble and poetic to the eyes of men, if pursued with sufficient buoyancy and freedom.

> "Tuesday," *A Week on the Concord and Merrimack Rivers*
> [*Writings* I.220]

Now the best works of art serve comparatively but to dissipate the mind, for they themselves represent transitionary and paroxysmal, not free and absolute, thoughts.

> Journal: July 1845 [*Writings VII.367–368*]

When on my way this afternoon, Shall I go down this long hill in the rain to fish in the pond? I ask myself. And I say to myself: Yes, roam far, grasp life and conquer it, learn much and live. Your fetters are knocked off; you are really free.

> Journal: 23 August 1845 [*Writings VII.385*]

As you know, I am not in any sense a politician. You who live in that snug and compact isle may dream of a glorious Commonwealth, but I have some doubts whether I and the new king of the Sandwich Islands shall pull together. When I think of the gold-diggers and the Mormons, the slaves and slave-holders, and the *flibustiers*, I naturally dream of a glorious *private life*. No—I am not patriotic; I shall not meddle with the gem of the Antilles; Gen. Quitman cannot count on my aid [in capturing Cuba], alas for him! nor can Gen. Pierce.

> Letter to Thomas Cholmondeley, 7 February 1855
> [*Correspondence 371*]

Men labor under a mistake; they are laying up treasures which moth and rust will corrupt and thieves break through and steal.

Northern Slavery, or the slavery which includes the Southern, Eastern, Western, and all others.

It is hard to have a Southern overseer; it is worse to have a Northern one; but worst of all when you are yourself the slave-driver. Look at the lonely teamster on the highway, wending to market by day or night; is he a son of the morning, with somewhat of divinity in him, fearless because immortal, going to receive his birthright, greeting the sun as his fellow, bounding with youthful, gigantic strength over his mother earth? See how he cowers and sneaks, how vaguely, indefinitely all the day he fears, not being immortal, not divine, the slave and prisoner of his own opinion of himself, fame which he has earned by his own deeds. Public opinion is a weak tyrant compared with private opinion. What I think of myself, that determines my fate.

Journal: 1845-1847 [*Writings VII. 427–428*]

Perhaps I am more than usually jealous with respect to my freedom. I feel that my connection with and obligation to society are still very slight and transient. Those slight labors which afford me a livelihood, and by which it is allowed that I am to some extent serviceable to my contemporaries, are as yet commonly a pleasure to me, and I am not often reminded that they are a necessity. So far I am successful. But I foresee that if my wants should be much increased, the labor required to supply them would become a drudgery. If I should sell both my forenoons and afternoons to society, as most appear to do, I am sure that for me there would be nothing left worth living for. I trust that I shall never thus sell my birthright for a mess of pottage.

"Life without Principle"
[*Writings IV. 460–461*]

We have all had our day-dreams, as well as more prophetic nocturnal vision; but as for farming, I am convinced that my genius dates from an older era than the agricultural. I would at least strike my spade into the earth with such careless freedom but accuracy as the woodpecker his bill into a tree. There is in my nature, methinks, a singular yearning toward all wildness.

> "Sunday," *A Week on the Concord and Merrimack Rivers*
> [*Writings* I.54]

I see young men, my townsmen, whose misfortune it is to have inherited farms, houses, barns, cattle, and farming tools; for these are more easily acquired than got rid of. Better if they had been born in the open pasture and suckled by a wolf, that they might have seen with clearer eyes what field they were called to labor in. Who made them serfs of the soil?

> "Economy," *Walden* [*Writings* II.5]

Farms are for sale all around here—and so, I suppose men are for purchase.

> Letter to Mr. and Mrs. John Thoreau, 8 June 1843
> [*Correspondence 114*]

But I would say to my fellows, once for all, As long as possible live free and uncommitted. It makes but little difference whether you are committed to a farm or the county jail.

> "Where I Lived, and What I Lived For," *Walden*
> [*Writings II.93*]

I tried to help him [John Field] with my experience, telling him that he was one of my nearest neighbors, and that I too, who came a-fishing here, and looked like a loafer, was getting my living like himself; that I lived in a tight, light, and clean house, which hardly cost more than the annual rent of such a ruin as his commonly amounts to; and how, if he chose, he might in a month or two build himself a palace of his own; that I did not use tea, nor coffee, nor butter, nor milk, nor fresh meat, and so did not have to work to get them; again, as I did not work hard, I did not have to eat hard, and it cost me but a trifle for my food; but as he began with tea, and coffee, and butter, and milk, and beef, he had to work hard to pay for them, and when he had worked hard he had to eat hard again to repair the waste of his system,—and so it was as broad as it was long, indeed it was broader than it was long, for he was discontented and wasted his life into the bargain; and yet he had rated it as a gain in coming to America, that here you could get tea, and coffee, and meat every day. But the only true America is that country where you are at liberty to pursue such a mode of life as may enable you to do without these, and where the state does not endeavor to compel you to sustain the slavery and war and other superfluous expenses which directly or indirectly result from the use of such things.

"Baker Farm," *Walden* [*Writings II.227–228*]

As I was leaving the Irishman's roof after the rain, bending my steps again to the pond, my haste to catch pickerel, wading in retired meadows, in sloughs and bog-holes, in forlorn and savage places, appeared for an instant trivial to me who had been sent to school and college; but as I ran down the hill toward the reddening west, with the rainbow over my shoulder, and some faint tinkling sounds borne to my ear through the cleansed air, from I know not what quarter, my Good Genius seemed to say,—

Go fish and hunt far and wide day by day,—farther and wider,—and rest thee by many brooks and hearth-sides without misgiving. Remember thy Creator in the days of thy youth. Rise free from care before the dawn, and seek adventures. Let the noon find thee by other lakes, and the night overtake thee everywhere at home. There are no larger fields than these, no worthier games than may here be played. Grow wild according to thy nature, like these sedges and brakes, which will never become English hay. Let the thunder rumble; what if it threaten ruin to farmers' crops? that is not its errand to thee. Take shelter under the cloud, while they flee to carts and sheds. Let not to get a living be thy trade, but thy sport. Enjoy the land, but own it not. Through want of enter-prise and faith men are where they are, buying and selling, and spending their lives like serfs.

"Baker Farm," *Walden* [*Writings II.229–230*]

Gardening is civil and social, but it wants the vigor and freedom of the forest and the outlaw.

"Sunday," *A Week on the Concord and Merrimack Rivers*
[*Writings I.55*]

I trust that the walkers of the present day are conscious of the blessings which they enjoy in the comparative freedom with which they can ramble over the country and enjoy the landscape, anticipating with compassion that future day when possibly it will be partitioned off into so-called pleasure-grounds, where only a few may enjoy the narrow and exclusive pleasure which is com-patible with ownership,—when walking over the surface of God's earth shall be construed to mean trespassing on some gentleman's grounds, when fences shall be multiplied and man traps and other engines invented to confine men to the public road. I am thankful that we have yet so much room in America.

Journal: 12 February 1851 [*Writings VIII. 156–157*]

Do we call this the land of the free? What is it to be free from King George the Fourth and continue the slaves of prejudice? What is it [to] be born free and equal, and not to live? What is the value of any political freedom, but as a means to moral freedom? Is it a freedom to be slaves or a freedom to be free, of which we boast? We are a nation of politicians, concerned about the outsides of freedom, the means and outmost defenses of freedom. It is our children's children who may perchance be essentially free. We tax ourselves unjustly. There is a part of us which is not represented. It is taxation without representation. We quarter troops upon ourselves. In respect to virtue or true manhood, we are essentially provincial, not metropolitan,—mere Jonathans. We are provincial, because we do not find at home our standards; because we do not worship truth but the reflection of truth; because we are absorbed in and narrowed by trade and commerce and agriculture, which are but means and not the end. We are essentially provincial, I say, and so is the English Parliament. Mere country bumpkins they betray themselves, when any more important question arises for them to settle. Their natures are subdued to what they work in!

Journal: 16 February 1851 [*Writings VIII. 162–163*]

He who lives according to the highest law is in one sense lawless. That is an unfortunate discovery, certainly, that of a law which binds us where we did not know that we were bound. Live free, child of the mist! He who for whom the law is made, who does not obey the law but whom the law obeys, reclines on pillows of down and is wafted at will whither he pleases, for man is superior to all laws, both of heaven and earth, when he takes his liberty.

Journal: 1851 [*Writings VIII. 171*]

"Free in this world, as the birds in the air, disengaged from every kind of chain." [*The Harivansa*]

Journal: 6 May 1851 [*Writings VIII. 191*]

1.30 A.M.—Full moon. Arose and went to the river and bathed, stepping very carefully not to disturb the household, and still carefully in the street not to disturb the neighbors. I did not walk naturally and freely till I had got over the wall.

Journal: 12 August 1851 [*Writings VIII. 383*]

There is some advantage, perhaps, in attending to the general features of the landscape over studying the particular plants and animals which inhabit it. A man may walk abroad and no more see the sky than if he walked under a shed. The poet is more in the air than the naturalist, though they may walk side by side. Granted that you are out-of-doors; but what if the outer door *is* open, if the inner door is shut! You must walk sometimes perfectly free, not prying nor inquisitive, not bent upon seeing things. Throw away a whole day for a single expansion, a single inspiration of air.

Journal: 21 August 1851 [*Writings VIII. 416*]

A cold and dark afternoon, the sun being behind clouds in the west. The landscape is barren of objects, the trees being leafless, and so little light in the sky for variety. Such a day as will almost oblige a man to eat his own heart. A day in which you must hold on to life by your teeth. You can hardly ruck up any skin on Nature's bones. The sap is down; she won't peel. Now is the time to cut timber for yokes and ox-bows, leaving the tough bark on,—yokes for your own neck. Finding yourself yoked to Matter and to Time.

Journal: 13 November 1851 [*Writings IX.110*]

I go to see many a good man or good woman, so called, and utter freely that thought which alone it was given me to utter; but there was a man who lived a long, long time ago, and his name was Moses, and another whose name was Christ, and if your thought does not, or does not appear to, coincide with what they said, the good man or the good woman has no ears to hear you.

Journal: 16 November 1851 [*Writings IX.119*]

We forget to strive and aspire, to do better ever than is expected of us. I cannot stay to be congratulated. I would leave the world behind me. We must withdraw from our flatterers, even from our friends. They drag us down. It is rare that we use our thinking faculty as resolutely as an Irishman his spade. To please our friends and relatives we turn out our silver ore in cartloads, while we neglect to work our mines of gold known only to ourselves far up in the Sierras, where we pulled up a bush in our mountain walk, and saw the glittering treasure. Let us return thither. Let it be the price of our freedom to make that known.

Journal: 13 January 1852 [*Writings IX.187–188*]

The thrush alone declares the immortal wealth and vigor that is in the forest. Here is a bird in whose strain the story is told, though Nature waited for the science of æsthetics to discover it to man. Whenever a man hears it, he is young, and Nature is in her spring. Wherever he hears it, it is a new world and a free country, and the gates of heaven are not shut against him. Most other birds sing from the level of my ordinary cheerful hours—a carol; but this bird never fails to speak to me out of an ether purer than that I breathe, of immortal beauty and vigor. He deepens the significance of all things seen in the light of his strain. He sings to make men take higher and truer views of things. He sings to amend their institutions; to relieve the slave on the plantation and the prisoner in his dungeon, the slave in the house of luxury and the prisoner of his own low thoughts.

Journal: 5 July 1852 [*Writings X.190–191*]

I must walk more with free senses.

Journal: 13 September 1852 [*Writings X.351*]

I love Nature partly *because* she is not man, but a retreat from him. None of his institutions control or pervade her. There a different kind of right prevails. In her midst I can be glad with an entire gladness. If this world was all man, I could not stretch myself, I should lose all hope. He is constraint, she is freedom to me. He makes me wish for another world. She makes me content with this. None of the joy she supplies is subject to his rules and definitions. What he touches he taints. In thought he moralizes. One would think that no free, joyful labor was possible to him.

Journal: 3 January 1853 [*Writings X.445*]

It is essential that a man confine himself to pursuits—a scholar, for instance, to studies—which lie next to and conduce to his life, which do not go against the grain, either of his will or his imagination. The scholar finds in his experience some studies to be most fertile and radiant with light, others dry, barren, and dark. If he is wise, he will not persevere in the last, as a plant in a cellar will strive toward the light. He will confine the observations of his mind as closely as possible to the experience or life of his senses. His thought must live with and be inspired with the life of the body. The death-bed scenes and observations even of the best and wisest afford but a sorry picture of our humanity. Some men endeavor to live a constrained life, to subject their whole lives to their wills, as he who said he would give a sign if he were conscious after his head was cut off,—but he gave no sign. Dwell as near as possible to the channel in which your life flows. A man may associate with such companions, he may pursue such employments, as will darken the day for him. Men choose darkness rather than light.

Journal: 12 March 1853 [*Writings XI. 16–17*]

The savage lives simply through ignorance and idleness or laziness, but the philosopher lives simply through wisdom. In the case of the savage, the accompaniment of simplicity is idleness with its attendant vices, but in the case of the philosopher, it is the highest employment and development. The fact for the savage, and for the mass of mankind, is that it is better to plant, weave, and build than do nothing or worse; but the fact for the philosopher, or a nation loving wisdom, is that it is most important to cultivate the highest faculties and spend as little time as possible in planting, weaving, building, etc. It depends upon the height of your standard, and no doubt through manual labor as a police men are educated up to a certain level. The simple style is bad for the savage because he does worse than to obtain the luxuries of life; it is good for the philosopher because he does better than to work for them. The question is whether you can bear freedom. At present the vast majority of men, whether black or white, require the discipline of labor which enslaves them for their good. . . But the philosopher does not require the same discipline; if he shovelled all day, we should receive no elevating suggestions from him.

Journal: 1 September 1853 [*Writings XI. 410–411*]

How watchful we must be to keep the crystal well that we were made, clear!—that it be not made turbid by our contact with the world, so that it will not reflect objects. What other liberty is there worth having, if we have not freedom and peace in our minds . . .

Journal: 26 October 1853 [*Writings XI. 453*]

For a year or two past, my *publisher*, falsely so called, has been writing from time to time to ask what disposition should be made of the copies of "A Week on the Concord and Merrimack Rivers" still on hand, and at last suggesting that he had use for the room they occupied in his cellar. So I had them all sent to me here, and they have arrived to-day by express, filling the man's wagon,— 706 copies out of an edition of 1000 which I bought of Munroe four years ago and have been ever since paying for, and have not quite paid for yet. The wares are sent to me at last, and I have an opportunity to examine my purchase. They are something more substantial than fame, as my back knows, which has borne them up two flights of stairs to a place similar to that to which they trace their origin. . . . I have now a library of nearly nine hundred volumes, over seven hundred of which I wrote myself. Is it not well that the author should behold the fruits of his labor? My works are piled up on one side of my chamber half as high as my head, my *opera omnia*. This is authorship; these are the work of my brain. . . . Nevertheless, in spite of this result, sitting beside the inert mass of my works, I take up my pen to-night to record what thought or experience I may have had, with as much satisfaction as ever. Indeed, I believe that this result is more inspiring and better for me than if a thousand had bought my wares. It affects my privacy less and leaves me freer.

Journal: 28 October 1853 [*Writings XI.459–460*]

I hate the present modes of living and getting a living. Farming and shopkeeping and working at a trade or profession are all odious to me. I should relish getting my living in a simple, primitive fashion. The life which society proposes to me to live is so artificial and complex—bolstered up on many weak supports, and sure to topple down at last—that no man surely can ever be inspired to live it, and only "old fogies" ever praise it. At best some think it their duty to live it. I believe in the infinite joy and satisfaction of helping myself and others to the extent of my ability. But what is the use in trying to live simply, raising what you eat, making what you wear, building what you inhabit, burning what you cut or dig, when those to whom you are allied insanely want and will have a thousand other things which neither you nor they can raise and nobody else, perchance, will pay for? The fellow-man to whom you are yoked is a steer that is ever bolting right the other way.

Journal: 5 November 1855 [*Writings XIV.7–8*]

I hear one thrumming a guitar below stairs. It reminds me of moments that I have lived. What a comment on our life is the least strain of music! It lifts me up above all the dust and mire of the universe. I soar or hover with clean skirts over the field of my life. It is ever life within life, in concentric spheres. The field wherein

I toil or rust at any time is at the same time the field for such different kinds of life! The farmer's boy or hired man has an instinct which tells him as much indistinctly, and hence his dreams and his restlessness; hence, even, it is that he wants money to realize his dreams with. The identical field where I am leading my humdrum life, let but a strain of music be heard there, is seen to be the field of some unrecorded crusade or tournament the thought of which excites in us an ecstasy of joy. The way in which I am affected by this faint thrumming advertises me that there is still some health and immortality in the springs of me. What an elixir is this sound! I, who but lately came and went and lived under *a dish cover*, live now under the heavens. It releases me; it bursts my bonds.

Journal: 13 January 1857 [*Writings XV.217*]

I say in my thought to my neighbor, who was once my friend, "It is of no use to speak the truth to you, you will not hear it. What, then, shall I say to you?" At the instant that I seem to be saying farewell forever to one who has been my friend, I find myself unexpectedly near to him, and it is our very nearness and dearness to each other that gives depth and significance to that forever. Thus I am a helpless prisoner, and these chains I have no skill to break. While I think I have broken one link, I have been forging another.

Journal: 23 February 1857 [*Writings XV.276*]

I saw at Ricketson's a young woman, Miss Kate Brady, twenty years old, her father an Irishman, a worthless fellow, her mother a smart Yankee. The daughter formerly did sewing, but now keeps school for a livelihood. She was born at the Brady house, I think in Freetown, where she lived till twelve years old and helped her father in the field. There she rode her horse to plow and was knocked off the horse by apple tree boughs, kept sheep, caught fish, etc., etc. I never heard a girl or woman express so strong a love for nature. She purposes to return to that lonely ruin, and dwell there alone, since her mother and sister will not accompany her; says that she knows all about farming and keeping sheep and spinning and weaving, though it would puzzle her to shingle the old house. There she thinks she can "live free."

Journal: 23 April 1857 [*Writings XV.335*]

They told me at New Bedford that one of their whalers came in the other day with a black man aboard whom they had picked up swimming in the broad Atlantic, without anything to support him, but nobody could understand his language or tell where he came from. He was in good condition and well-behaved. My respect for my race rose several degrees when I heard this, and I thought they had found the true merman at last. "What became of him?" I inquired. "I believe they sent him to the State Almshouse," was the reply. Could anything have been more ridiculous? That he should be beholden to Massachusetts for his support who floated free where Massachusetts with her State Almshouse could not have supported herself for a moment.

Journal: 23 April 1857 [*Writings XV.337*]

I ordinarily plod along a sort of whitewashed prison entry, subject to some indifferent or even grovelling mood. I do not distinctly realize my destiny. I have turned down my light to the merest glimmer and am doing some task which I have set myself. I take incredibly narrow views, live on the limits, and have no recollection of absolute truth. Mushroom institutions hedge me in. But suddenly, in some fortunate moment, the voice of eternal wisdom reaches me even, in the strain of the sparrow, and liberates me, whets and clarifies my senses, makes me a competent witness.

Journal: 12 May 1857 [*Writings XV.364–365*]

The thinker, he who is serene and self-possessed, is the brave, not the desperate soldier. He who can deal with his thoughts as a material, building them into poems in which future generations will delight, he is the man of the greatest and rarest vigor, not sturdy diggers and lusty polygamists. He is the man of energy, in whom subtle and poetic thoughts are bred. Common men can enjoy partially; they can go a-fishing rainy days; they can *read* poems perchance, but they have not the vigor to beget poems. They can enjoy feebly, but they cannot create. Men talk of freedom! How many are free to think? free from fear, from perturbation, from prejudice? Nine hundred and ninety-nine in a thousand are perfect slaves. How many can exercise the highest human faculties? He is the man truly—courageous, wise, ingenious—who can use his thoughts and ecstacies as the material of fair and durable creations. One man shall derive from the fisherman's story more than the fisher has got who tells it. The mass of men do not know how to cultivate the fields they traverse. The mass glean only a scanty pittance where the thinker reaps an abundant harvest. What is all your building, if you do not build with thoughts? No exercise implies more real manhood and vigor than joining thought to thought. How few men can tell what they have thought! I hardly know half a dozen who are not too lazy for this. They cannot get over some difficulty, and therefore they are on the long way round. You conquer fate by thought. If you think the fatal thought of men and institutions, you need never pull the trigger. The consequences of thinking inevitably follow. There is no more Herculean task than to think a thought about this life and then get it expressed.

Journal: 6 May 1858 [*Writings XVI. 404–405*]

Preaching? Lecturing? Who are ye that ask for these things? What do ye want to hear, ye puling infants? A trumpet-sound that would train you up to mankind, or a nurse's lullaby? The preachers and lecturers deal with men of straw, as they are men of straw themselves. Why, a free-spoken man, of sound lungs, cannot draw a long breath without causing your rotten institutions to come toppling down by the vacuum he makes. Your church is a baby-house made of blocks, and so of the state. It would be a relief to breathe one's self occasionally among men. If there were any magnanimity in us, any grandeur of soul, anything but sects and parties undertaking to patronize God and keep the mind within bounds, how often we might encourage and provoke one another by a free expression! I will not consent to walk with my mouth muzzled, not till I am rabid, until there is danger that I shall bite the unoffending and that my bite will produce hydrophobia.

Freedom of speech! It hath not entered into your hearts to conceive what those words mean. It is not leave given me by your sect to say this or that; it is when leave is given to your sect to withdraw. The church, the state, the school, the magazine, think they are liberal and free! It is the freedom of a prison-yard. I ask only that one fourth part of my honest thoughts be spoken aloud.

Journal: 16 November 1858 [*Writings XVII.324*]

It is no compliment to be invited to lecture before the rich Institutes and Lyceums. . . .

There is the Lowell Institute with its restrictions, requiring a certain faith in the lecturers. How can any free-thinking man accept its terms? . . .

They want all of a man but his truth and independence and manhood.

Journal: 16 November 1858 [*Writings XVII.327–329*]

Look at your editors of popular magazines. I have dealt with two or three the most liberal of them. They are afraid to print a whole sentence, a *round* sentence, a free-spoken sentence.

Journal: 16 November 1858 [*Writings XVII.325*]

It is the uncivilized free and wild thinking in Hamlet and the Iliad, in all the scriptures and mythologies, not learned in the schools, that delights us. As the wild duck is more swift and beautiful than the tame, so is the wild—the mallard—thought, which 'mid falling dews wings its way above the fens.

"Walking" [*Writings V.231*]

We believe that Carlyle has, after all, more readers, and is better known to-day for this very originality of style, and that posterity will have reason to thank him for emancipating the language, in some measure, from the fetters which a merely conservative, aimless, and pedantic literary class had imposed upon it, and setting an example of greater freedom and naturalness.

"Thomas Carlyle and His Works" [*Writings IV.330*]

Carlyle is not a *seer*, but a brave looker-on and *reviewer*; not the most free and catholic observer of men and events, for they are likely to find him preoccupied, but unexpectedly free and catholic when they fall within the focus of his lens.

"Thomas Carlyle and His Works" [*Writings IV.342*]

The poet... makes us free of his hearth and heart, which is greater than to offer one the freedom of a city.

"Friday," *A Week on the Concord and Merrimack Rivers*
[*Writings I.362–363*]

Poetry is the only life got, the only work done, the only pure product and free labor of man, performed only when he has put all the world under his feet, and conquered the last of his foes.

"Thomas Carlyle and His Works" [*Writings IV.344*]

The poet will write for his peers alone. He will remember only that he saw truth and beauty from his position, and expect the time when a vision as broad shall overlook the same field as freely.

"Friday," *A Week on the Concord and Merrimack Rivers*
[Writings I.363]

If a man is thought-free, fancy-free, imagination-free, that which *is not* never for a long time appearing *to be* to him, unwise rulers or reformers cannot fatally interrupt him.

"Civil Disobedience" [*Writings IV.383*]

How rarely I meet with a man who can be free, even in thought! We live according to rule. Some men are bedridden; all, world-ridden. I take my neighbor, an intellectual man, out into the woods and invite him to take a new and absolute view of things, to empty clean out of his thoughts all institutions of men and start again; but he can't do it, he sticks to his traditions and his crotchets. He thinks that governments, colleges, newspapers, etc., are from everlasting to everlasting.

Journal: 12 May 1857 [*Writings XV.362*]

> I make ye an offer,
> Ye gods, hear the scoffer,
> The scheme will not hurt you,
> If ye will find goodness, I will find virtue.
> Though I am your creature,
> And child of your nature,
> I have pride still unbended,
> And blood undescended,
> Some free independence,
> And my own descendants.
> I cannot toil blindly,
> Though ye behave kindly,
> And I swear by the rood,
> I'll be slave to no God.
> If ye will deal plainly,
> I will strive mainly,
> If ye will discover,
> Great plans to your lover,
> And give him a sphere
> Somewhat larger than here.

"Sunday," *A Week on the Concord and Merrimack Rivers*
[*Writings I.69–70*]

In short, all good things are wild and free.

"Walking" [*Writings V.234*]

If you are ready to leave father and mother, and brother and sister, and wife and child and friends, and never see them again,—if you have paid your debts, and made your will, and settled all your affairs, and are a free man, then you are ready for a walk.

"Walking" [*Writings V.206*]

We have felt that we almost alone hereabouts practiced this noble art; though, to tell the truth, at least if their own assertions are to be received, most of my townsmen would fain walk sometimes, as I do, but they cannot. No wealth can buy the requisite leisure, freedom, and independence which are the capital in this profession. It comes only by the grace of God.

"Walking" [*Writings V.206–207*]

I think that I cannot preserve my health and spirits, unless I spend four hours a day at least—and it is commonly more than that—sauntering through the woods and over the hills and fields, absolutely free from all worldly engagements.

"Walking" [*Writings V.207*]

Eastward I go only by force; but westward I go free. Thither no business leads me. It is hard for me to believe that I shall find fair landscapes or sufficient wildness and freedom behind the eastern horizon.

"Walking" [*Writings V.217*]

Live free, child of the mist,—and with respect to knowledge we are all children of the mist. The man who takes the liberty to live is superior to all the laws, by virtue of his relation to the lawmaker. "That is active duty," says the Vishnu Purana, "which is not for our bondage; that is knowledge which is for our liberation: all other duty is good only unto weariness; all other knowledge is only the cleverness of an artist."

"Walking" [*Writings V.240–241*]

During the berry season the schools have a vacation, and many little fingers are busy picking these small fruits. It is ever a pastime, not a drudgery. I remember how glad I was when I was kept from school a half a day to pick huckleberries on a neighboring hill all by myself to make a pudding for the family dinner. Ah, they got nothing but the pudding, but I got invaluable experience beside! A half a day of liberty like that was like the promise of life eternal. It was emancipation in New England.

Journal: 16 July 1851 [*Writings VIII.308*]

I have come out this afternoon a-cranberrying, chiefly to gather some of the small cranberry, *Vaccinium Oxycoccus*...This was a small object, yet not to be postponed, on account of imminent frosts, *i.e.*, that is, if I would know this year the flavor of the European cranberry as compared with our larger kind. I thought I should like to have a dish of this sauce on the table at Thanksgiving of my own gathering. I could hardly make up my mind to come this way, it seemed so poor an object to spend the afternoon on. I kept foreseeing a lame conclusion,—how I should cross the Great Fields, look into Beck Stow's Swamp, and then retrace my steps no richer than before. In fact, I expected little of this walk, yet it did pass through the side of my mind that somehow, on this very account (my small expectation), it would turn out well, as also the advantage of having some purpose, however small, to be accomplished— of letting your deliberate wisdom and foresight in the house to some extent direct and control your steps. If you would really take a position outside the street and daily life of men, you must have deliberately planned your course, you must have business which is not your neighbors' business, which they cannot understand. For only absorbing employment prevails, succeeds, takes up space, occupies territory, determines the future of individuals and states, drives Kansas out of your head, and actually and permanently occupies the only desirable and free Kansas against all border ruffians. The attitude of resistance is one of weakness, inasmuch as it only faces an enemy; it has its back to all that is truly attractive. You shall have your affairs, I will have mine. You will spend this afternoon in setting up your neighbor's stove, and be paid for it; I will spend it in gathering the few berries of the *Vaccinium Oxycoccus* which Nature produces here, before it is too late, and *be paid for it also* after another fashion. I have always reaped unexpected and incalculable advantages from carrying out at last, however tardily, any little enterprise which my genius suggested to me long ago as a thing to be done,—some step to be taken, however slight, out of the usual course.

Journal: 30 August 1856 [*Writings: XV.35–36*]

At present, in this vicinity, the best part of the land is not private property; the landscape is not owned, and the walker enjoys comparative freedom. But possibly the day will come when it will be partitioned off into so-called pleasure-grounds, in which a few will take a narrow and exclusive pleasure only,—when fences shall be multiplied, and man-traps and other engines invented to confine men to the *public* road, and walking over the surface of God's earth shall be construed to mean trespassing on some gentleman's grounds. To enjoy a thing exclusively is commonly to exclude yourself from the true enjoyment of it. Let us improve our opportunities, then, before the evil days come.

"Walking" [*Writings V.216*]

The Brahman Saradwata, says the Dharma Sacontala, was at first confounded on entering the city, "but now," says he, "I look on it as the freeman on the captive, as a man just bathed in pure water on a man smeared with oil and dust."

Journal: 6 May 1851 [*Writings VIII.193*]

I rarely walk by moonlight without hearing—the sound of a flute, or a horn, or a human voice. It is a performer I never see by day; should not recognize him if pointed out; but you may hear his performance in every horizon. He plays but one strain and goes to bed early, but I know by the character of that single strain that he is deeply dissatisfied with the manner in which he spends his day. He is a slave who is purchasing his freedom. He is Apollo watching the flocks of Admetus on every hill, and this strain he plays every evening to remind him of his heavenly descent. It is all that saves him,—his one redeeming trait.

Journal: 5 August 1851 [*Writings VIII.373*]

Ah, yes, even here in Concord horizon Apollo is at work for King Admetus! Who is King Admetus? It is Business, with his four prime ministers Trade and Commerce and Manufactures and Agriculture.

Journal: 6 August 1851 [*Writings VIII.378*]

Men are such confirmed arithmeticians and slaves of business that I cannot easily find a blank-book that has not a red line or a blue one for the dollars and cents, or some such purpose.

Journal: 21 August 1851 [Writings VIII.414]

The river flows in the rear of the towns, and we see all things from a new and wilder side. The fields and gardens come down to it with a frankness, and freedom from pretension, which they do not wear on the highway.

"A Winter Walk" [Writings V.178]

INDEPENDENCE

My life more civil is and free
　　Than any civil polity.

Ye princes, keep your realms
　　And circumscribèd power,
Not wide as are my dreams,
　　Nor rich as is this hour.

What can ye give which I have not?
What can ye take which I have got?
　　Can ye defend the dangerless?
　　Can ye inherit nakedness?

To all true wants Time's ear is deaf,
Penurious states lend no relief
　　Out of their pelf:
　　But a free soul—thank God—
　　Can help itself.

Be sure your fate
  Doth keep apart its state,
Not linked with any band,
  Even the nobles of the land;

In tented fields with cloth of gold
  No place doth hold,
But is more chivalrous than they are,
  And sigheth for a nobler war;
A finer strain its trumpet rings,
A brighter gleam its armor flings.

The life that I aspire to live
  No man proposeth me;
No trade upon the street
  Wears its emblazonry.

[Writings 415–416]

The mass of men serve the state thus, not as men mainly, but as machines, with their bodies. They are the standing army, and the militia, jailers, constables, *posse comitatus*, etc. In most cases there is no free exercise whatever of the judgment or of the moral sense; but they put themselves on a level with wood and earth and stones; and wooden men can perhaps be manufactured that will serve the purpose as well.

"Civil Disobedience" *[Writings IV.359]*

Under a government which imprisons any unjustly, the true place for a just man is also a prison. The proper place to-day, the only place which Massachusetts has provided for her freer and less desponding spirits, is in her prisons, to be put out and locked out of the State by her own act, as they have already put themselves out by their principles. It is there that the fugitive slave, and the Mexican prisoner on parole, and the Indian come to plead the wrongs of his race should find them; on that separate, but more free and honorable, ground, where the State places those who are not *with* her, but *against* her,—the only house in a slave State in which a free man can abide with honor. If any think that their influence would be lost there, and their voices no longer afflict the ear of the State, that they would not be as an enemy within its walls, they do not know by how much truth is stronger than error, nor how much more eloquently and effectively he can combat injustice who has experienced a little in his own person. Cast your whole vote, not a strip of paper merely, but your whole influence. A minority is powerless while it conforms to the majority; it is not even a minority then; but it is irresistible when it clogs by its whole weight. If the alternative is to keep all just men in prison, or give up war and slavery, the State will not hesitate which to choose.

"Civil Disobedience" [*Writings IV.370–371*]

When I converse with the freest of my neighbors, I perceive that, whatever they may say about the magnitude and seriousness of the question, and their regard for the public tranquillity, the long and the short of the matter is, that they cannot spare the protection of the existing government, and they dread the consequences to their property and families of disobedience to it.

"Civil Disobedience" [*Writings IV.373*]

It is evident that a private man is not worth so much in Canada as in the United States, and if that is the bulk of a man's property, *i.e.* the being private and peculiar, he had better stay here. An Englishman, methinks, not to speak of other nations, habitually regards himself merely as a constituent part of the English nation; he holds a recognized place as such; he is a member of the royal regiment of Englishmen. And he is proud of his nation. But an American cares very little about such, and greater freedom and independence are possible to him.

Journal: 18 August 1851 [*Writings VIII.399*]

I have paid no poll-tax for six years. I was put into a jail once on this account, for one night; and, as I stood considering the walls of solid stone, two or three feet thick, the door of wood and iron, a foot thick, and the iron grating which strained the light, I could not help being struck with the foolishness of that institution which treated me as if I were mere flesh and blood and bones, to be locked up. I wondered that it should have concluded at length that this was the best use it could put me to, and had never thought to avail itself of my services in some way. I saw that, if there was a wall of stone between me and my townsmen, there was a still more difficult one to climb or break through before they could get to be as free as I was. I did not for a moment feel confined, and the walls seemed a great waste of stone and mortar.

"Civil Disobedience" [*Writings IV.375*]

Our legislators have not yet learned the comparative value of free trade and of freedom, of union, and of rectitude, to a nation.

"Civil Disobedience" [*Writings IV.386*]

There will never be a really free and enlightened State until the

State comes to recognize the individual as a higher and independent power, from which all its own power and authority are derived, and treats him accordingly. I please myself with imagining a State at last which can afford to be just to all men, and to treat the individual with respect as a neighbor; which even would not think it inconsistent with its own repose if a few were to live aloof from it, not meddling with it, nor embraced by it, who fulfilled all the duties of neighbors and fellow-men. A State which bore this kind of fruit, and suffered it to drop off as fast as it ripened, would prepare the way for a still more perfect and glorious State, which also I have imagined, but not yet anywhere seen.

"Civil Disobedience" [*Writings IV.387*]

When I sat on Lee's Cliff the other day (August 29th), I saw a man working with a horse in a field by the river, carting dirt; and the horse and his relation to him struck me as very remarkable. There was the horse, a mere animated machine,—though his tail was brushing off the flies,—his whole existence subordinated to the man's, with no tradition, perhaps no instinct, in him of independence and freedom, of a time when he was wild and free,—completely humanized. No compact made with him that he should have the Saturday afternoons, or the Sundays, or any holidays. His independence never recognized, it being now quite forgotten both by men and by horses that the horse was ever free. For I am not aware that there are any wild horses known surely not to be descended from tame ones. Assisting that man to pull down that bank and spread it over the meadow; only keeping off the flies with his tail, and stamping, and catching a mouthful of grass or leaves from time to time, on his own account,—all the rest for man. It seemed hardly worth while that he should be *animated* for this. It was plain that the man was not educating the horse; not trying to develop his nature, but merely getting work out of him. That mass of animated matter seemed more completely the servant of man than any inanimate. For slaves have their holidays; a heaven is conceded to them, but to the horse none. Now and forever he is man's slave. The more I considered, the more the man seemed akin to the horse; only his was the stronger will of the two. For a little further on I saw an Irishman shoveling, who evidently was as much tamed as the horse. He had stipulated that to a certain extent his independence be recognized, and yet really he was but little more independent. I had always instinctively regarded the horse as a free people somewhere, living wild. Whatever has not come under the sway of man is wild. In this sense original and independent men are wild,—not tamed and broken by society. Now for my part I have such a respect for the horse's nature as would tempt me to let him alone; not to interfere with him,—his walks, his diet, his loves. But by mankind he is treated simply as if he was an engine which must have rest and is sensible of pain. Suppose that every squirrel were made to turn a coffee-mill! Suppose that the gazelles were made to draw milk-carts?

There he was with his tail cut off, because it was in the way, or to suit the taste of his owner; his mane trimmed, and his feet shod with iron that he might wear longer. What is a horse but an animal that has lost its liberty? What is it but a system of slavery? and do you not thus by *insensible* and unimportant degrees come to human slavery? Has lost its liberty!—and has man got any more liberty himself for having robbed the horse, or has he lost just as much of his own, and become more like the horse he has robbed? Is not the other end of the bridle in this case, too, coiled round his own neck?

Journal: 3 September 1851 [*Writings VIII. 447–448*]

I rejoice that horses & steers have to [be] *broken* before they can be made the slaves of men, and that men themselves have some wild oats still left to sow before they become submissive members of society. Undoubtedly all men are not equally fit subjects for civilization, and because the majority, like dogs and sheep, are tame by inherited disposition, is no reason why the others should have their natures broken, that they may be reduced to the same level. Men are in the main alike, but they were made several in order that [they] might be various. If a low use is to be served, one man will do nearly or quite as well as another; if a high one, individual excellence is to be regarded. Any man can stop a hole to keep the wind away, but no other man can serve that use which the author of this illustration did.

                          Journal: 6 May 1851 [*Writings VIII. 192*]

We saw last summer, on the side of a mountain, a dog employed to churn for a farmer's family, traveling upon a horizontal wheel, and though he had sore eyes, an alarming cough, and withal a demure aspect, yet their bread did get buttered for all that. Undoubtedly, in the most brilliant successes, the first rank is always sacrificed. Much useless traveling of horses, *in extenso,* has of late years been improved for man's behoof, only two forces being taken advantage of,—the gravity of the horse, which is the centripetal, and his centrifugal inclination to go ahead. Only these two elements in the calculation. And is not the creature's whole economy better economized thus? Are not all finite beings better pleased with motions relative than absolute? And what is the great

114 THOREAU ON FREEDOM

globe itself but such a wheel,—a larger tread-mill,—so that our horse's freest steps over prairies are oftentimes balked and rendered of no avail by the earth's motion on its axis? But here he is the central agent and motive-power; and, for variety of scenery, being provided with a window in front, do not the ever-varying activity and fluctuating energy of the creature himself work the effect of the most varied scenery on a country road? It must be confessed that horses at present work too exclusively for men, rarely men for horses; and the brute degenerates in man's society.

"Paradise (To Be) Regained" [*Writings IV.285–286*]

I have heard of a horse which his master could not catch in his pasture when the first snowflakes were falling, who persisted in wintering out. As he persisted in keeping out of his reach, his master finally left him. When the snow had covered the ground three or four inches deep, the horse pawed it away to come at the grass,—just as the wild horses of Michigan do, who are turned loose by their Indian masters,—and so he picked up a scanty sub-sistence. By the next day he had had enough of free life and pined for his stable, and so suffered himself to be caught.

Journal: 20 June 1850 [*Writings VIII.37–38*]

FREE LOVE

My love must be as free
  As is the eagle's wing,
Hovering o'er land and sea
  And every thing.

I must not dim my eye
　　In thy saloon,
I must not leave my sky
　　And nightly moon.

Be not the fowler's net
　　Which stays my flight,
And craftily is set
　　T' allure the sight.

But be the favoring gale
　　That bears me on,
And still doth fill my sail
　　When thou art gone.

I cannot leave my sky
　　For thy caprice,
True love would soar as high
　　As heaven is.

The eagle would not brook
　　Her mate thus won,
Who trained his eye to look
　　Beneath the sun.

[*The Dial*, (October 1842) 199]

Yet we think that if rail fences are pulled down, and stone walls
piled up on our farms, bounds are henceforth set to our lives
and our fates decided. If you are chosen town clerk, forsooth,
you cannot go to Tierra del Fuego this summer: but you may

go to the land of infernal fire nevertheless.

"Conclusion," *Walden* [*Writings II.352*]

Most men, even in this comparatively free country, through mere ignorance and mistake, are so occupied with the factitious cares and superfluously coarse labors of life that its finer fruits cannot be plucked by them.

"Economy," *Walden* [*Writings II.6*]

The necessaries of life for man in this climate may, accurately enough, be distributed under the several heads of Food, Shelter, Clothing, and Fuel; for not till we have secured these are we prepared to entertain the true problems of life with freedom and a prospect of success.

"Economy," *Walden* [*Writings II.13*]

I also have in my mind that seemingly wealthy, but most terribly impoverished class of all, who have accumulated dross, but know not how to use it, or get rid of it, and thus have forged their own golden or silver fetters.

"Economy," *Walden* [*Writings II.18*]

In those days when how to get my living honestly, with freedom left for my proper pursuits, was a question which vexed me even more than it does now, I used to see a large box by the railroad, six feet long by three wide, in which the workmen locked up their tools at night; and it suggested to me that every man who was hard pushed might get him such a one for a dollar, and having bored a few auger-holes in it, to admit the air at least, get into it when it rained and at night, and shut the lid and hook it, and so have freedom in his mind, and in his soul be free. This did not seem the worst alternative, nor by any means a despicable resource. You could sit up as late as you pleased; and, whenever you got up in the morning, you would not have any creditor dogging you for rent. I should not be in a bad box. Many a man is harassed to death to pay the rent of a larger and more luxurious box, who would not have frozen to death in such a box as this. I should not be in so bad a box as many a man is in now.

Journal: 28 January 1852 [*Writings IX.240–241*]

The farmer is endeavoring to solve the problem of a livelihood by a formula more complicated than the problem itself. To get his shoestrings he speculates in herds of cattle. With consummate skill he has set his trap with a hair springe to catch comfort and independence, and then, as he turned away, got his own leg into it. . . . And when the farmer has got his house, he may not be the richer but the poorer for it, and it be the house that has got him. As I understand it, that was a valid objection urged by Momus against the house which Minerva made, that she "had not made it movable, by which means a bad neighborhood might be avoided;" and it may still be urged, for our houses are such unwieldy property that we are often imprisoned rather than housed in them; and the bad neighborhood to be avoided is our own scurvy selves. I know one or two families, at least, in this town, who, for nearly a generation, have been wishing to sell their houses in the outskirts and move into the village, but have not been able to accomplish it, and only death will set them free.

"Economy," *Walden* [*Writings II.36–37*]

By avarice and selfishness, and a grovelling habit, from which none of us is free, of regarding the soil as property, or the means of acquiring property chiefly, the landscape is deformed, husbandry is degraded with us, and the farmer leads the meanest of lives.

"The Bean-Field," *Walden* [*Writings II.183*]

I would rather ride on earth in an ox cart, with a free circulation, than go to heaven in the fancy car of an excursion train and breathe a *malaria* all the way.

"Economy," *Walden* [*Writings II.41*]

If I seem to boast more than is becoming, my excuse is that I brag for humanity rather than for myself; and my shortcomings and inconsistencies do not affect the truth of my statement. Notwithstanding much cant and hypocrisy,—chaff which I find it difficult to separate from my wheat, but for which I am as sorry as any man,—I will breathe freely and stretch myself in this respect, it is such a relief to both the moral and physical system; and I am resolved that I will not through humility become the devil's attorney. I will endeavor to speak a good word for the truth.

"Economy," *Walden* [*Writings II.55*]

I am wont to think that men are not so much the keepers of herds as herds are the keepers of men, the former are so much the freer.

"Economy," *Walden* [*Writings II.62*]

This town is said to have the largest houses for oxen, cows, and horses hereabouts, and it is not behindhand in its public buildings; but there are very few halls for free worship or free speech in this county.

"Economy," *Walden* [*Writings II.63*]

I cannot but feel compassion when I hear some trig, compact-looking man, seemingly free, all girded and ready, speak of his "furniture," as whether it is insured or not.

"Economy," *Walden* [*Writings II. 73*]

For more than five years I maintained myself thus solely by the labor of my hands, and I found that, by working about six weeks in a year, I could meet all the expenses of living. The whole of my winters, as well as most of my summers, I had free and clear for study.

"Economy," *Walden* [*Writings II. 76*]

As I preferred some things to others, and especially valued my freedom, as I could fare hard and yet succeed well, I did not wish to spend my time in earning rich carpets or other fine furniture, or delicate cookery, or a house in the Grecian or the Gothic style just yet. If there are any to whom it is no interruption to acquire these things, and who know how to use them when acquired, I relinquish to them the pursuit. Some are "industrious," and appear to love labor for its own sake, or perhaps because it keeps them out of worse mischief; to such I have at present nothing to say. Those who would not know what to do with more leisure than they now enjoy, I might advise to work twice as hard as they do,—work till they pay for themselves, and get their free papers. For myself I found that the occupation of a day-laborer was the most independent of any, especially as it required only thirty or forty days in a year to support one. The laborer's day ends with the going down of the sun, and he is then free to devote himself to his chosen pursuit, independent of his labor; but his employer, who speculates from month to month, has no respite from one end of the year to the other.

In short, I am convinced, both by faith and experience, that to maintain one's self on this earth is not a hardship but a pastime, if we will live simply and wisely; as the pursuits of the simpler nations are still the sports of the more artificial. It is not necessary that a man should earn his living by the sweat of his brow, unless he sweats more easier than I do.

"Economy," *Walden* [*Writings II.78*]

A man has his price at the South, is worth so many dollars, and so he has at the North. Many a man here sets out by saying, I will make so many dollars by such a time, or before I die, and that is his price, as much as if he were knocked off for it by a Southern auctioneer.

Journal: 29 November 1860 [*Writings XX.284*]

There are a thousand hacking at the branches of evil to one who is striking at the root, and it may be that he who bestows the largest amount of time and money on the needy is doing the most by his mode of life to produce that misery which he strives in vain to relieve. It is the pious slave-breeder devoting the proceeds of every tenth slave to buy a Sunday's liberty for the rest.

"Economy," *Walden* [*Writings II.84*]

Children come a-berrying, railroad men taking a Sunday morning walk in clean shirts, fishermen and hunters, poets and philosophers; in short, all honest pilgrims, who came out to the woods for freedom's sake, and really left the village behind, I was ready to greet with,—"Welcome, Englishmen! welcome, Englishmen!" for I had had communication with that race.

"Visitors," *Walden* [*Writings II.170*]

After hoeing, or perhaps reading and writing, in the forenoon, I usually bathed again in the pond, swimming across one of its coves for a stint, and washed the dust of labor from my person, or smoothed out the last wrinkle which study had made, and for the afternoon was absolutely free.

"The Village," *Walden* [*Writings II.185*]

It is remarkable how many creatures live wild and free though secret in the woods, and still sustain themselves in the neighborhood of towns, suspected by hunters only.

"Brute Neighbors," *Walden*
[*Writings II.252*]

Walden, being like the rest usually bare of snow, or with only shallow and interrupted drifts on it, was my yard where I could walk freely when the snow was nearly two feet deep on a level elsewhere and the villagers were confined to their streets.

"Winter Animals," *Walden*
[*Writings II.299–300*]

We need the tonic of wildness. . . We can never have enough of nature. We must be refreshed by the sight of inexhaustible vigor, vast and titanic features, the sea-coast with its wrecks, the wilderness with its living and its decaying trees, the thunder-cloud, and the rain which lasts three weeks and produces freshets. We need to witness our own limits transgressed, and some life pasturing freely where we never wander.

"Spring," *Walden* [*Writings II.350*]

The town's poor seem to me often to live the most independent lives of any. Maybe they are simply great enough to receive without misgiving.

"Conclusion," Walden [Writings II.361]

Thank God, no Hindoo tyranny prevailed at the framing of the world, but we are freemen of the universe, and not sentenced to any caste.

"Monday," A Week on the Concord and Merrimack Rivers
[Writings I.155]

Just before sundown we reached some more falls in the town of Bedford, where some stone-masons were employed repairing the locks in a solitary part of the river. They were interested in our adventure, especially one young man of our own age, who inquired at first if we were bound up to "'Skeag;" and when he had heard our story, and examined our outfit, asked us other questions, but temperately still, and always turning to his work again, though as if it were become his duty. It was plain that he would like to go with us, and, as he looked up the river, many a distant cape and wooded shore were reflected in his eye, as well as in his thoughts.

"Tuesday," A Week on the Concord and Merrimack Rivers
[Writings I.247–248]

Art is not tame, and Nature is not wild, in the ordinary sense. A perfect work of man's art would also be wild or natural in a good sense. Man tames Nature only that he may at last make her more free even than he found her, though he may never yet have succeeded.

"Thursday," A Week on the Concord and Merrimack Rivers
[Writings I.337]

What is produced by a free stroke charms us, like the forms of lichens and leaves.

"Thursday," *A Week on the Concord and Merrimack Rivers*
[*Writings I.351*]

The bird of paradise is obliged constantly to fly against the wind, lest its gay trappings, pressing close to its body, impede its free movements.

"Friday," *A Week on the Concord and Merrimack Rivers*
[*Writings I.362*]

It is not every man who can be a Christian, even in a very moderate sense, whatever education you give him. It is a matter of constitution and temperament, after all. He may have to be born again many times. I have known many a man who pretended to be a Christian, in whom it was ridiculous, for he had no genius for it. It is not every man who can be a free man, even.

"The Last Days of John Brown"
[*Writings IV.445*]

Now I yearn for one of those old, meandering, dry, uninhabited roads, which lead away from towns, which lead us away from temptation, which conduct to the outside of earth, over its uppermost crust; where you may forget in what country you are traveling; where no farmer can complain that you are treading down his grass, no gentleman who has recently constructed a seat in the country that you are trespassing; on which you can go off at half-cock and wave adieu to the village; along which you may travel like a pilgrim, going nowhither; where travellers are not too often to be met; where my spirit is free . . .

There I have freedom in my thought, and in my soul am free.

Journal: 21 July 1851 [*Writings VIII.322, 325*]

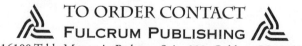